365 TV-free

Activities for Toddlers

Di Hodges

HINKLER
BOOKS

Published in 2002 by Hinkler Book Pty Ltd

17–23 Redwood Drive

Dingley VIC 3172 Australia

www.hinklerbooks.com

Reprinted 2003

© Hinkler Books Pty Ltd 2002

Written by: Di Hodges
Edited by: Julie Haydon

ISBN: 1 8651 5722 8

Printed & bound in Australia.

CONTENTS

FOREWORD

Like many parents, you probably consider that your children spend far too much time watching TV or playing on the computer. Recent research has shown that these are the most popular recreational activities for children outside school hours. This has contributed to major concerns in our community regarding the high levels of obesity in our children, which are directly related to sitting down in front of the TV or computer rather than kicking a ball around or being involved in other active play.

While we all know that the TV or computer can be great learning tools, countless studies have shown that children learn best from 'doing'. The second-hand experiences they gain from watching the TV or playing on the computer will never replace what children learn through their play and through 'hands-on' experience.

This book is designed to help you get your children involved in a host of exciting activities. Activities to enhance their creativity, increase their knowledge of the world around them, develop their coordination, boost their self-confidence and to provide them with lots of good old-fashioned fun!

While some of the activities require adult participation, others only need a parent's help to get the children started. Safety is of the utmost importance though, and activities using objects such as scissors or knives should be closely supervised.

Turn off the TV or computer and spend some quality time with your children working on the activities in this book. This will help them develop their imaginations and improve their communication skills and stand them in good stead in the years ahead.

*

Di Hodges has been an early childhood teacher for over twenty years. She has taught in a variety of settings, including pre-schools, prep classes and years 1 and 2. She has also spent many years helping geographically isolated parents teach their pre-schoolers at home through Distance Education facilities.

Di has a Diploma of Teaching for Early Childhood and Primary, and a Bachelor of Education. She is currently an Education Advisor (Pre-school) with Education Queensland.

HOW TO USE THIS BOOK

This book is full of ideas that you can enjoy trying with your 1 to 4-year-old children. Each page contains a short list of materials you will need to collect before you begin the activity. More often than not these are everyday household items you will already have. Save junk, as many activities in this book use recycled household junk. Other materials may need to be purchased from newsagents, craft shops or your local discount store.

This book contains two indexes—a subject index at the front of the book and an alphabetical activity index at the back. The book is divided into ten categories:

Indoor Activities
Let's Create
Food Fun
Word Play
Number Games
Games to Play
Outdoor Activities
Exploring the Environment
Sports Skills
Special Occasions

The activities in each category of the book have been divided into age groups from 1 to 4-year-olds and sorted alphabetically. There will be something that is exactly right for your child. The suggested age on each activity is a guide only—remember that all children are different and you'll soon know if an activity is too easy or too difficult for your child.

Start with easy activities, give lots of praise and then move on to harder activities.

This book will help you find those areas of learning that your child needs extra time and help with. Don't forget that to succeed at school and in life, our children need a healthy self-image and parents can foster this with lots of praise, encouragement, time and love. Have fun together!

GUIDE TO SYMBOLS

These simple symbols give a quick visual reference to the basic elements present in each activity.

 Outdoor activity: This symbol indicates an outdoor activity.

 Indoor activity: This symbol indicates an indoor activity. **Note:** If both symbols are present, the activity can be enjoyed both outdoors and indoors.

 Adult participation: This activity requires some degree of adult supervision. Read the 'What To Do' closely, to see the degree of monitoring required. This symbol can also indicate that participation with an adult is important for learning or sharing.

 Pencils, paints and paper: This activity requires basic drawing or painting tools. It can be as simple as a pencil and paper for keeping score in a game, or art materials for decorating etc.

 Tools required: This activity requires tools of some type. This could be anything from a simple bowl and vegetable peeler, to balloons and craft materials. Most activities have been designed to use basic everyday items found in the home, such as cereal boxes. Some activities may require items to be purchased, but they should be inexpensive or alternatives can be used. Read the 'What You Need' for specific items. Adult supervision is required.

 Learning and imagination: Just about all of the activities in this book encourage imaginative play. There are activities that require some adult participation and may contain important learning skills, designed for fun. If the activity is simply a game to occupy a bored child, this symbol will not be present.

The symbols indicated in this book are a guide only. It is the responsibility of all adults to determine the appropriate activities for each child and the skills they possess. The use of tools requires adult supervision.

INDOOR ACTIVITIES

DETERGENT BOX BLOCKS

*Junk materials often make the best play toys for young children,
and by recycling packaging you are saving money and the environment.*

What You Need

- Square laundry detergent cartons
- Masking tape • Coloured or patterned adhesive plastic

What To Do

Many laundry detergents now come in block-shaped cartons. They make ideal building blocks for your children. After wiping them out, tape the lids closed with masking tape and then cover with coloured or patterned plastic (can be bought by the metre from most hardware stores.)

Store the blocks neatly in the largest basket you can buy and add to the supply as you wash! My son uses his for building towers, making cities to go with his train set, making castles, and so on.

Challenge your children to a competition to see who can build the highest tower before it falls down. If you have toddlers they will love it if older children build towers for them to knock down!

MAGAZINE PICTURE PUZZLES

Create simple jigsaw puzzles with your children from large magazine pictures.

What You Need

- Large magazine pictures • Scissors
- Glue • Thick pieces of cardboard

What To Do

Look through magazines with your children and let them choose some pictures they would like to make into puzzles. Help them cut out the pictures, then use a strong glue to stick the pictures onto thick pieces of cardboard.

When the glue is dry, cut the picture into puzzle shapes. With younger children begin with four or five puzzle pieces. As they master the skill, cut the pictures into more pieces.

Store and label the puzzles in plastic lunch bags in a shoebox.

1+

STORYTIME

*Teach your children the joys of reading from an early
age and they will thank you for it in later life.*

What You Need
- Books • Time

What To Do

It is never too early to interest your children in books and reading. Literacy is a vital skill and an appreciation of books from an early age can give your children a great start to learning, and be a lifetime source of pleasure.

There is a huge variety of excellent children's literature available, either to buy or borrow from your local library. Set aside some time each day to sit with your children and read them a story. Younger children enjoy looking at books with large, bright images. Older children will enjoy memorising simple stories and rhymes, and will follow along as you read together, often repeating parts of the story.

Have patience with very young children when they ask you to read the same book over and over again. Take time to show them the words, as well as the pictures.

Many local libraries also have 'storytime' sessions for toddlers and pre-schoolers. They are a great way to interest even the youngest child in books and reading.

SURPRISE BAGS

There are many times when you will have to keep your young children amused and quiet—in an aeroplane or train, visiting someone in hospital, or perhaps just in a waiting room. Surprise bags are great for times like these.

What You Need

• Fabric bag • Interesting things to put inside it

What To Do

Make or buy a fabric bag to hold the surprises. Collect things as you see them and have a bag ready to take with you when you need it in a hurry.

Some suggestions for things to put in the bag are:

A new book to read together
Notebook or scribbling block
Packet of coloured pipe-cleaners
Large wooden beads and plastic thread for threading
Peggi-beads and board for building towers
A new jigsaw puzzle stored in a plastic bag
Threading cards
Finger puppet
Magnifying glass
New small toy or car
Unbreakable mirror

BASH A BAG

Let your young children use up some energy with this simple activity.

What You Need

- A bag made of strong paper, plastic or fabric
- String • Newspaper • Wooden spoon

What To Do

Your children will love helping you tear up the newspaper and roll it into balls to fill the punching bag. When the bag's full, tie it tightly with string. Hang the bag from a hook or doorway. (Make sure it will not hit anything precious.)

Your children will have a great time bashing away at the bag with a wooden spoon. Make sure they take it in turns and don't hit each other by accident!

BOX FUN

A creative way to have lots of good cheap fun!

What You Need

- Cardboard fruit boxes of all sizes • Props such as cardboard cylinders, broom handles, sheets, rugs • Masking tape

What To Do

On wet days when the children are driving you crazy, drive to your local fruit shop and ask if you can have some fruit boxes. They are usually happy to let you load up as many as you can fit in your car. Let the kids loose with the boxes and their imaginations, and they will spend hours making tunnels, cubbies, towers and other creations.

When they have lost interest in building cubbies, save the boxes to make box cars or enlist their help to tidy up their toys and store some away in boxes for other rainy days.

DRESS-UPS

Dressing up is an important part of young children's play. Provide a variety of dressing-up clothes for them and they will play happily for hours.

What You Need

- Cardboard box • Old magazines • Scissors • Glue
- Variety of dressing-up clothes and props

What To Do

Have your children decorate a cardboard box to hold the dressing-up things.

Collect clothes and props to put in the box. Relatives may have hats, wigs, beads and old clothes to donate. Sometimes a visit to an opportunity shop can yield wonderful (but cheap!) dressing-up clothes. When choosing accessories and clothes make sure they can be put on easily and worn safely. You may have to take up hems, thread elastic through waistbands to make them smaller, and perhaps even replace tiny buttons and fasteners with Velcro. This way, their dressing-up play need not always involve an adult.

The dressing-up collection might include necklaces, bangles, clip-on earrings, shorts, T-shirts, coats, trousers, ties, belts, dresses, skirts (the frillier the better), lacy nighties, petticoats, pantihose, stockings, tights, shoes, boots, handbags, purses, wallets, scarves, shawls and glasses (without the lenses).

INDOOR OBSTACLE COURSE

*Going through an obstacle course helps develop
body coordination, control and balance.*

What You Need

• Furniture • Cord • Pillows • Towels • Rug • Balloons
• Small beanbags • Socks • Household items

What To Do

On wet days when the kids are going 'stir crazy' set up an indoor obstacle course. (Make sure precious ornaments are safely out of the way first!)

Some ideas:

Crawling through the legs of the kitchen chairs
Crawling under a coffee table (watch those heads!)
Sliding under (on their tummies) a cord tied between two chairs
Making a tunnel out of chairs, cushions and a rug
Playing leapfrog—stepping from towel to towel (on carpet so they don't slip)
Crawling through balloons that are tied under a table without moving any
Walking along a 'balance beam' made of rolled-up towels

Let older children try the course balancing a small beanbag on their heads, or holding a sock in each hand.

Time the children to see who completes the course in the shortest time. Graph the results together.

KITCHEN PLAY

As well as helping you in the kitchen with simple tasks, toddlers love playing make-believe with some of your kitchen gadgets.

What You Need

- Unbreakable bowls, spoons, ladles, baking trays, muffin tins, measuring spoons, plastic jugs and cups • Playdough or water
- Food colouring • Large plastic sheet or plastic tablecloth • Felt pen

What To Do

On a hot day your children will love 'cooking' outside with water—measuring, stirring, pouring and mixing. Add a few drops of food colouring to the water and they will think it's great!

On cooler days, spread the plastic sheet on the ground, give the children some playdough and the kitchen items and they will 'cook' happily for ages. A cardboard carton turned on its side makes a great pretend stove. Draw some 'hotplates' on the top with a felt pen and put a biscuit rack inside for the oven shelves.

SILLY WALKING

This has been a favourite bedtime routine with our young child for some time.

What You Need

- Time

What To Do

Bedtime routines vary in all families, but 'silly walking' is one we use that I thought I would share with you. If you bring routines into bedtime, it often makes putting young children down for the night easier.

When it's bedtime my child and I take it in turns to be the leader for 'silly walking'. As we go through the house playing 'follow the leader', he gets ready for bed—a stop for a small drink of water in the kitchen, a stop to kiss Dad in the lounge, a toilet stop, and then a stop to brush his teeth in the bathroom. Then he happily snuggles down in bed for a bedtime story and goodnight kiss!

BALLOON BOUNCING

An activity to help your children learn their body parts and improve their coordination.

What You Need

- A blown-up balloon for each child

What To Do

Encourage your children to toss their balloons in the air and keep them from touching the floor. Count with the children to see how many times they can tap their balloons before they come down.

Encourage your children to keep their balloons up by using other parts of the body—head, elbows, knees, feet, back etc.

Challenge your children further by seeing if they can:

Keep two balloons up at once
Lie on the floor and keep the balloon up with their feet
Hop on one foot and use their knee to bounce the balloon
Jump around holding the balloon between their knees

BOTTLES AND LIDS

This activity will help develop your children's powers of prediction as they guess which lid fits which bottle. It's also a good way to develop the muscles in their hands and fingers.

What You Need

- Bottles of different shapes and sizes with screw-top lids

What To Do

Put out a selection of jars (at least ten) with lids with different circumferences. See if your children can find the correct lid for each jar and screw it on.

Later, they might like to time themselves with an egg timer to see how fast they can do it.

They could also put the jars in order from the smallest lid to the largest.

Hint!

Have your children do this activity on a mat or carpet rather than on a hard floor. Remind them to take great care with the glass bottles.

DRESSING FAST

This game will give your children practice dressing themselves.

What You Need

- Dressing-up clothes

What To Do

Set up two piles of similar clothes—maybe a shirt, a pair of long pants, socks and a hat each. Pick two children to stand beside you. When you say 'go', they must each run to a pile of clothes, put them on over their own clothes, and do up all the buttons and fasteners. Then they run back to you.

Don't forget to have a camera handy! This game is lots of fun at birthday parties, as well as being terrific practice for doing up buttons, clips and zips.

If you are playing it with your children on their own, they can try to beat the clock, or use an egg timer.

FOOTPRINTS

A fun way to help teach your children right and left.

What You Need

- Cardboard • Pens
- Scissors • Blu-Tack

What To Do

Have one child stand on a piece of cardboard. Draw around the left foot and cut the footprint out. Use this shape as a template and make at least ten more. Do the same with the right foot. Give your children cutting practice by letting them help you cut out the shapes.

Blu-Tack the feet in a walking pattern around the house and have your children follow them.

If you like, you can make it a treasure hunt with a surprise at the end!

Vary the difficulty by placing the footprints further apart, or by having a hopping section.

MEMORY

A fun way to develop your children's memories.

What You Need

- Assortment of small items such as a pencil, rubber, scissors, pen, small toys, hair brush, cutlery • Tray • Tea towel
- Paper and pencil (for older children who can write)

What To Do

For younger children—place a few items on the tray and let your children look at them for a minute. Have your children turn their backs while you remove a couple of items from the tray and cover them with a tea towel. Ask your children to turn around and look at the tray and tell you what's missing.

For older children—place up to twenty items on the tray and cover them up. Uncover them in front of your children and give them a minute to try and memorise the items, then cover them up again. Your children then write down as many items as possible.

Have a turn yourself and see if your memory is better than your children's. You may be unpleasantly surprised!

MISMATCH

A family game to see how observant everyone is.

What You Need

- Two or more players

What To Do

If the whole family plays, divide into two teams. If just a few people play, one person at a time has a turn.

The first player or team leaves the room. The other team or players mismatch five things around the room—perhaps put some cushions on the floor instead of the couch, turn an ornament upside down, put someone's shoes on their hands instead of their feet, or put a T-shirt on inside out. I am sure you will think of plenty to do.

When the player or team returns, they have to spot the five mismatches. For any they do not notice, the other player or team scores a point.

The next player or team then has a turn. The player or team with the most points is the winner.

ODD ONE OUT

Help your children understand the meaning of same and different.

What You Need

- Pairs of matching objects, such as a pair of socks, a pair of shoes, two matching mugs, two matching forks

What To Do

Mix up the items and have your children find the two that are the same. Then ask them to cover their eyes. Put a pair of matching objects together with one that is different. Your children have to find the odd one out and tell you why it doesn't belong.

Make this game more difficult by making the differences more subtle.

RICE MARACAS

Children love making music. Make some simple rice maracas with them and they will love playing them and following the beat of their favourite songs.

What You Need

- Paper cups • Uncooked rice
- Masking or insulating tape • Felt pens

What To Do

Fill a paper cup about half full of uncooked rice and then place an empty cup on the top. Your children can help hold the cups firmly and steadily in place while you join them together with tape. Now they can use their felt pens to decorate the maracas in bright colours.

Make maracas with different amounts of rice. For different sound effects you could use dried pasta, beans or split peas.

Shake out some different rhythms and see if they can copy them.

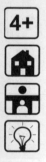

ANIMAL SHADOWS

Lots of fun and a great way to develop the imagination.

What You Need

• Lamp • Hands

What To Do

Shine a light on to a wall in your children's darkened room. Try and make as many different sorts of animal shadows on the wall with your hands as you can. Start with simple ones and see if you and your children can create some more, or try some of the ones listed below.

Butterfly
Pig
Camel
Hare

For children who are frightened of shadows and who often think they 'see' strange things in a room at night, this game might make them less afraid of the dark.

COIN CLEANING

Children love collecting and handling coins—and cleaning them!

What You Need

- Bowl of water • Bar of soap • Old toothbrush
- Coins • Old tea towel or clean rag

What To Do

Have your children drop the coins in the bowl of water. Each child removes one coin and rubs it with the bar of soap, then the toothbrush. They dip the coin in the water, and polish it with an old tea towel or rag.

Your children will be delighted by how new their shiny coins look.

COIN SORTING

This activity will help familiarise your children with different coins.

What You Need

- Lots of coins of different denominations

What To Do

Give your children a pile of coins of different denominations. Ask the children to sort the coins into piles.

They can sort the coins by:

Colour e.g. silver, gold
Value e.g. put all the ten-cent pieces together, all the twenty-cent pieces together
Size

Discuss what we do with money and how coins differ from notes.

FUNNY FEET

Make some 'funny feet' with your children for them to wear and add to their dressing-up box. Watch the imaginative games begin.

What You Need

- Egg cartons • Scissors • Rubber bands • Rubber gloves
- Strong cardboard • Pair of old socks

What To Do

You can make a variety of 'funny feet' or just one pair.

Cut two egg cartons in half, then cut off the tops. Cut triangular shapes around the sides of the tops so they look like claws. Your children can attach them to their feet (or hands) with rubber bands. Hey presto! Instant tigers!

Let your children wear old rubber gloves on the ends of their feet, so they can be a platypus, seal or duck.

Make clown feet by putting some strong cardboard inside a pair of old socks.

4+

NEWSPAPER WALK

A good indoor game to play with the whole family.
(But don't play on the carpet or the newsprint may mark it!)

What You Need

- Two or more players
- Two pieces of newspaper per player

What To Do

Mark out a starting and finishing line. Each player stands on the starting line with their two pieces of paper in front of them. When you say 'go', the players must get to the finishing line without touching the floor. To do this they must walk on one piece of paper and then put the other piece in front of them. They then pick up the first piece, place that down in front, and walk on that.

The first player to reach the finishing line by only walking on their pieces of newspaper is the winner. The children love watching Mum and Dad have a go at this too, so go on, be a good sport and give them a laugh. Think how good all the bending is for the waistline!

NUTS AND BOLTS

4+

Another thinking-ahead and predicting activity. This game will also help your children learn how to screw and unscrew bolts—great for developing the hand and finger muscles needed for writing.

What You Need

- A selection of different-sized screws with nuts they will screw into

What To Do

Give your children at least a dozen different-sized bolts and matching nuts. See if they can find the ones that go together, then ask them to screw the nuts into the bolts.

To increase the challenge they might like to:

Beat the clock—time them and see if they can beat their PB (personal best)
Beat an egg timer
Do it blind-folded
Time each other or another family member and see who is the fastest

4+

PAPER-BAG PUPPETS

Help your children make a collection of paper-bag puppets,
then they can put on a puppet show for the rest of the family.

What You Need

• Paper bags • Glue • Scissors • Felt pens
• Scrap paper or other collage materials

What To Do

Today, most supermarket bags are made of plastic, but some stores are becoming environmentally conscious and are again using large brown paper bags. These make fantastic puppets. Otherwise buy a pack of brown paper lunch bags.

Your children can make their puppets any way they like, but perhaps they might like to cut or tear long strips of coloured paper for hair, add a cellophane mouth and draw large eyes. Don't forget that the bottom of the puppet is where the hand goes in! Older children may like to make funny faces using photos cut from magazines.

When the puppets are finished, your children put their hands in the bags and make the puppets talk!

Fat puppets are fun to make, too. Stuff the paper bag with newspaper and insert a long cardboard cylinder. Make sure the cylinder is long enough to stick out of the bottom of the bag. Staple or sticky tape the cylinder in place. Hold the puppet by the cylinder and make it move.

PLAYING SHOPS

4+

*Solve the problem of wet-day boredom by helping
your children set up a 'pretend shop'.*

What You Need

- Large cardboard cartons or small table • Items for the shop
  • Blu-Tack • Coins • Paper • Crayons • Scissors
  • Props such as plastic bags, toy cash register,
  plastic shopping trolley

What To Do

Help your children make a shop with cardboard cartons or a table. Raid the pantry together for tins and packets they can borrow for the shop.

To make money, Blu-Tack some coins to the table, place a piece of paper over them and show them how to rub over the coins with a crayon to get the coin rubbings. Help the children cut them out. If they have a toy cash register they can use that for the shop, otherwise help them find a container for the takings.

Make a shopping list and visit their shop—they'll love serving Mum!

LET'S
CREATE

BLACKBOARDS

Blackboards are great for young children.
They make a terrific gift from grandparents.

What You Need

- A strong and stable blackboard
- A variety of chalk sticks

What To Do

Set your children up with a good quality blackboard and they will use it for years.

Blackboards are best if they are large enough to allow young children to draw using wide arm movements. You can make your own blackboard by painting a wall or a large, flat piece of wood with blackboard paint.

Having a blackboard will provide many opportunities for your children to draw and write.

Hint!

It's best to use blackboards outside so that the dust can be hosed off.

CHALK DRAWINGS

*Buy some thick sticks of chalk for the children to
draw on the pavers or the concrete outside.*

What You Need

- Thick sticks of coloured chalk
- Room to draw outside • A hose

What To Do

You can now buy lovely thick sticks of coloured chalk for pavement drawing. The children will enjoy creating beautiful pictures outside with their coloured chalks. They could draw on the pavers, concrete, or even the brick walls of the house. Best of all, it is easily cleaned off with the hose.

Hint!

Make sure your children understand that they can only do this with chalk. Pens, crayons and felt pens are not so easy to remove!

COLOURFUL BLOB PAINTINGS

Children are always surprised and delighted by blob paintings.

What You Need

- Paper • Brushes • Colourful paints (acrylic paint works well, or make up a strong paint with wallpaper paste and food dyes)

What To Do

Help your child fold her sheet of paper in two. Open the sheet, then show her how to put blobs of paint on one side of the paper. Fold the paper over and press it down hard. When she opens up the paper—wow! What is it? Maybe it's a butterfly or a monster! Anything is possible with a child's imagination.

When the blob painting is dry, she can draw around the picture and cut it out.

EDIBLE PLAYDOUGH

Make some simple edible playdough that younger children will enjoy playing with.

What You Need

- Peanut paste • Milk powder
- Sugar • Edible food colouring

What To Do

Younger children often want to eat regular playdough. If this is happening with your younger children, put away the regular playdough until they are older and can understand not to eat it, and make them a batch of edible playdough.

Simply mix one part of peanut paste to one part of milk powder and half a part of sugar. Double or triple the quantities depending on how much you want. Add some food colouring if desired.

PAINT POTS

1+

A cheap outdoor activity to do on a sunny day.

What You Need

- Buckets or empty tins • Water
- Food colouring • Paintbrushes

What To Do

Young children love painting, but it is not always possible or practical to provide real paints. They also love painting with real brushes like Mum and Dad.

Half fill each bucket or tin with water and add some food colouring. Give each child a paintbrush. Now the children can 'paint' the paths, driveway, concrete, or even the outside of the house, and you can rest easy knowing it can all be hosed off later!

PHOTO PUZZLES

Make some simple cheap puzzles for your children to put together.

What You Need

- Large photos of your children, family or home
- Craft glue • Strong cardboard
- Clear adhesive plastic (or have the photos laminated)
- Scissors or a craft knife

What To Do

Use large photos that you already have or have some enlarged cheaply at your local photocopying shop. Your children will love doing a puzzle of their face, their whole body, one of the family, or perhaps their bedroom. Just use your imagination, or ask them!

Use craft glue to paste the photos onto the cardboard. When they are dry, plastic over both sides or take them to be laminated. Then use scissors or a craft knife to cut them into large puzzle pieces. As your children gain mastery of the puzzles, you can cut them into smaller pieces to increase the challenge.

Take photos of some of your friends' children and make them individual puzzles too—great cheap gifts, and everyone will be amazed at your creativity!

PRINTING PLAYDOUGH

Printing playdough is a simple activity that gives children the opportunity to explore new materials.

What You Need

- Playdough (see p46)
- Materials for printing, such as flowers, gumnuts, kitchen items, leaves, nuts and bolts, old keys, parts of the body such as toes, fingers and elbows, toy blocks, stones

What To Do

Show your children how to make interesting patterns and prints in their playdough with a selection of the materials suggested above.

BOX CARS

Making cheap play props like this helps develop your child's imagination.

What You Need

- Cardboard box • Scissors • Acrylic paint • Glue
- Paper plates, pieces of cardboard, aluminium pie plates
- Felt pens • Rope

What To Do

Make a box car for your children. Cut the flaps off the top and bottom of a cardboard box, except for the flap at the front. Your children can paint the box at this stage—maybe racy red, or British racing green! When it's done, stick paper plates on the side for wheels and aluminium pie dishes on the front for headlights. Make straps out of rope. The children step inside their box cars and slip the straps over their shoulders. Now they're off and racing!

BREAKFAST-CEREAL THREADINGS

Breakfast-cereal loops can make pretty necklaces and bracelets, and children love to make them. Threading is also an excellent hand-eye coordination activity.

What You Need

- Bodkin or a large tapestry needle • Wool
- Breakfast-cereal loops

What To Do

Help your children thread their needles or bodkins with wool and tie a cereal loop at the end of the wool to secure it. If you don't want your younger children using needles, wrap some sticky tape around the end of the wool to make a firm threading and they can thread with that.

Older children will enjoy making colourful patterns as they thread. Younger ones will enjoy eating their creations at the end!

2+

BUSY BOX

Make a Busy Box with your children.

What You Need

- Strong cardboard box with a lid (apple boxes are ideal)
- Children's paintings, magazine pictures, wrapping paper etc.
- Glue • Paper • Acrylic paints or crayons

What To Do

Help your children decorate their busy box. You could use some of their paintings or drawings, magazine pictures, wrapping paper or magazine illustrations to collage all over the box. Alternatively, they could paint it with bright acrylic paints or, after covering it with white paper, they could decorate it with crayons or felt pens.

Find a suitable place to store the busy box that's easily accessible for everyone—perhaps in a wardrobe or in the bottom of your linen cupboard.

In the box keep a shoebox that contains the 'tools of the trade'—good-quality children's scissors (children will easily become frustrated with learning to cut if scissors aren't sharp), sticky tape in a good-quality dispenser, masking tape, glue bottle or glue pen, and a stapler. A pencil case should hold crayons, felt pens and coloured pencils. Add whatever else you and your children would like to your busy box (see p45).

BUSY-BOX COLLECTION

Here are some suggestions for junk, art, and collage materials you may like to collect and store in the Busy Box. Some smaller materials will be best stored in individual containers (margarine or takeaway containers make ideal small storage containers).

What You Need

- Aluminium foil, beads, bottle tops, bark, cardboard, cylinders (lunch wraps and toilet rolls), cellophane, chalk, chocolate wrappers, confetti, corks, cotton reels, cotton wool, dried flowers, egg cartons, egg shells, fabric scraps, feathers, grasses, gift wrappings, glitter, ice-cream sticks, leather scraps, leaves, old toothbrushes, paint sample sheets, paper, paper bags, paper clips, patty pans, pebbles, pine cones, pipe-cleaners, ribbons, rulers, sandpaper, seeds, sequins, scraps of lace, sawdust, straws, styrofoam, stickers, sponges, string, sweets wrappers, toothpicks, wallpaper samples or off-cuts, wool and yarn, anything else you can think of

What To Do

I've included this activity because having a collection of art materials and junk on hand is a necessity for many of the activities in this book. Children are natural recyclers and our junk is often their treasure!

COLOURFUL PLAYDOUGH

2+

Make up a batch of simple cooked playdough for your children. It will keep them occupied for ages and provide a great outlet for their creativity.

What You Need

- 1 cup plain flour • 1 cup water • $\frac{1}{2}$ cup cooking salt
- 1 tablespoon cream of tartar • 1 tablespoon cooking oil
- Food colouring or powder paints • Wooden spoon
- Saucepan • Breadboard • Plastic containers

What To Do

With a wooden spoon, mix the flour, water, salt and cream of tartar in a saucepan over a medium heat until thick. When it has cooled, add the oil and knead well on a floured board.

Divide the dough into at least six balls and add a different colour to each ball until you have blue, red, yellow, green, purple and orange playdough. (If you want plain playdough, omit the colouring.)

Put each colour into a separate container and encourage your children to create playdough pictures or dioramas. When they have finished, help them sort out the colours to put back in their containers for another day, rather than mixing them all together. Happy modelling!

CREATIVE PLAYDOUGH

Playing with playdough gives children the opportunity to be creative while developing their finger muscles—so important for writing at school!

What You Need

- Playdough (see p46)
- Objects to use with the playdough
e.g. baking trays, biscuit and scone cutters,
cake and muffin tins, garlic crushers,
ice-cream sticks, old keys, patty pans,
pipe-cleaners, plastic cutlery,
plastic hammers, plastic scissors,
potato mashers, rolling pins, tea strainers

What To Do

Make up a batch of playdough with your children and give them all or a selection of the items mentioned above. They will play happily for ages. Make sure you are close by to admire their creations and to try making some of your own.

FACE PAINTING

Children love having their faces painted and it is always a very popular activity at birthday parties.

What You Need

- Towel • Face paints or sorbelene cream mixed with powder paints
- Long make-up brushes • Cotton buds • Face glitter • Mirror

What To Do

Mix non-toxic powder paints with sorbelene cream. Cover each child with a towel and apply the face paint with make-up brushes or cotton buds.

Children usually have lots of ideas for characters, but some suggestions are fairies, cats and butterflies, or action figures like Batman and Spider-Man.

A wash of white paint over the face makes the colours stand out, and some face glitter at the end looks really pretty.

Practise your skills and you'll soon be in demand for parties! Older children are great at face painting, too!

FEET PAINTING

Feet painting is a fun alternative to finger painting. Children love the squishy, slimy feeling as they draw with their feet.

What You Need

- 2 tablespoons cornflour • Cold water
- 1 cup boiling water • Food colouring
- Saucepan • Wooden spoon
- Large sheet of plastic or plastic tablecloth

What To Do

Blend the cornflour with a little cold water and mix to a smooth paste. Add the boiling water and stir over a low heat until the mixture thickens. Add some food colouring and mix thoroughly.

Cover an outdoor area with a large sheet of plastic or a plastic tablecloth. Let the children draw pictures in the paint with their feet.

Make sure there is a bucket of warm soapy water handy for cleaning up.

FINGER PAINTING

Finger painting provides a wonderful sensory experience for children of all ages.

What You Need

- 2 tablespoons cornflour • Cold water
- 1 cup boiling water • Food colouring
- Saucepan • Wooden spoon
- Large sheet of plastic or plastic tablecloth

What To Do

Blend the cornflour with a little cold water and mix to a smooth paste. Add the boiling water and stir over a low heat until the mixture thickens. Add some food colouring and mix thoroughly.

Cover an outdoor table with a large sheet of plastic or a plastic tablecloth, or use a table that can be hosed or washed down. Alternatively, spread the plastic on the grass or on pavers and the children can finger paint there.

Younger children will enjoy just drawing pictures in the paint and will love the squishy feeling of the finger paint. Older children might enjoy using some combs, grout scrapers or thick cardboard cut into comb shapes to make interesting patterns.

If they want to keep a finger-painting picture you can take a print by carefully pushing a piece of paper onto the picture and then lifting it off slowly.

GREEN DAY

A great way to teach colours to young children.

What You Need

- Green items such as clothing, food, drinks, toys, paint

What To Do

Tell your children in the morning that you are going to have a 'green day' or whatever colour takes your fancy. Use your imagination to make it as exciting as you can.

Some possibilities are:

Add a small amount of green food colouring to their milk

Select green foods to try, such as avocado, celery pieces, green apple, honeydew melon, kiwi fruit, snow peas

Select green clothes for everyone to wear

Cook green foods, such as avocado dip, green jelly, green cordial iceblocks, patty cakes with green icing

Make a batch of playdough and colour half yellow and half blue so your children can see it change to green as they play

Add some yellow and blue food colouring to their bath water and watch it turn green

Be 'greenies' and do lots of gardening, maybe plant some seeds

Go to a park and collect lots of different leaves for leaf rubbings at home with green crayons and pencils

Make and use some green paint

Read 'Green Eggs and Ham' at bedtime

HOBBY HORSES

Children love pretending. Make a hobby horse with your
little ones and it will be a favourite pet for years.

What You Need

- A long cardboard cylinder or a broom handle
- Acrylic paints • Paintbrushes • Large sock
- Filling such as fabric scraps, paper, old pantihose
- Coloured permanent felt pens • Glue
- Wool • Cord or thin rope

What To Do

Paint the cardboard cylinder or broom handle. Let your children help. They will enjoy choosing the colours for their own special horse.

Stuff the foot of the sock with filling, then decorate it to look like a horse's head. Use permanent pens and sew or glue on some wool for the mane.

Next, slip the sock onto the cylinder or broom handle and tie it on securely with a cord or thin rope. Use part of the cord or rope to make reins and the 'horse' is ready for naming and riding.

MARBLE PAINTINGS

2+

Make colourful wrapping paper using paint-covered marbles.

What You Need

- Plain paper • Shirt or cereal boxes or a large plastic box
- Marbles • Containers of coloured paints • Teaspoons

What To Do

Put the paper in a large box and drop a few marbles into each paint container. Use a teaspoon to lift out one marble at a time and put it in the box on top of the paper. Now show your children how to tilt the box to roll the paint-covered marble all around the box. Keep doing this until all the paint has come off the marble and made marble tracks over the paper.

Change marbles and repeat until the paper is covered with bright tracks of colour.

Hint!

Use the marble paintings as wrapping paper.

PAPER-BAG KITES

Your littlies will love making a paper-bag kite to use on windy days.

What You Need

- Paper bags • Crayons, coloured pencils or felt pens
- Crepe paper • Scissors • Stapler or sticky tape
- Masking tape • Hole punch • String

What To Do

Help the children decorate their paper bags. Make sure they're really bright and colourful. Attach some crepe-paper strips with a stapler or some sticky tape to the closed ends of the paper bags. These are the tails of the kites.

On one side of the open ends of the bags place some masking tape for reinforcement, and then punch a hole in the masking tape. Thread some string through the hole to complete each kite.

These kites will not fly up in the air, but your children will have lots of fun running with their kites flying behind them in the wind. If you don't have enough room at home, pack a picnic and take them to a large park where they can run and play safely with their kites.

PET ROCKS

An oldie but a goldie!

What You Need

- Smooth creek or riverbed rocks
- Paints or collage materials

What To Do

Next time you're walking near a creek or river, help your children select some lovely smooth rocks to bring home for 'pets'. Younger children will be especially enchanted with this idea.

At home your children can decorate their pet rocks with paint, or glue on collage materials— perhaps some wool for hair, a button for a nose, a ricrac braid mouth, and so on.

A pet rock makes a great paperweight and is a very easy pet to look after!

RIBBON STICKS

Make some beautiful ribbon sticks to add some colour to the children's day.
Your children will love waving their ribbon sticks in time to music or as they dance.

What You Need

- Coloured satin ribbons 7 m x 5 cm (23 ft x 2 in)
- Dowel pieces 50 cm x 1.25 cm (20 in x 0.5 in)
  - Needle and thread • Metal eyelets
  - Eye screw • Fishing tackle swivels

What To Do

Double over the first metre of each length of ribbon and sew together. Sew the head of the ribbon into an arrow shape. Sew a metal eyelet into the top of this arrow shape.

Screw an eye screw into a length of the dowel and attach one of the swivels to this. Connect the swivel to the metal eyelet and the ribbon will twist and swivel on the dowel as the child swings the stick.

Hint!

The sticks will look even prettier if they are painted or decorated. Your children will love helping with this.

SAND MOULDS

Young children love making imprints in damp sand with sand moulds.

What You Need

- Sand moulds • Sandpit or beach visit
- Objects such as kitchen utensils, small toys, blocks

What To Do

Sand moulds make terrific gifts for small fry and are very cheap to buy at chain stores or toy shops. However, it is easy to find lots of items around the home that make interesting sand moulds. (For example, kitchen utensils, baking dishes with patterns, small toys and construction blocks all make interesting patterns in sand.)

Find a selection of objects to use to make imprints. Ask your children to close their eyes (no peeping) while you make an imprint with one of the items. Then see who can find the item that made the imprint.

Play until the children are sick of the game and then reverse it and see if they can trick you!

2+

SPONGE SHAPES

Make bath time extra special by creating some homemade bath sponges in the shapes of your children's favourite animals.

What You Need

- Sheet of foam sponge about 5 cm (2 in) thick
  - Pencil • Tracing paper • Marker pen
    - Scissors or craft knife

What To Do

First, ask your children what shape they would like their sponges to be. Then have them help find pictures of the shapes they want in one of their books or a magazine.

Place the tracing paper over the images and trace around them with a pencil. Then cut them out. If they are small images, it is a good idea to photocopy them and enlarge them before cutting them out (your local library will have a photocopier with this capability).

Now place the tracing paper over the sponge and trace around the edges of the shapes with the marker pen. Use the scissors or craft knife to cut the sponge shapes out. The sponge shapes are now ready for the bath!

Important!

Always remember that children should be closely supervised whenever they are near water.

TEXTURED PLAYDOUGH

2+

*Introduce your children to new textures by adding
interesting materials to playdough.*

What You Need

- Playdough recipe (see p46)
- Sand • Rice • Confetti
- Split peas • Lentils • Dried beans
- Glitter or small leaves

What To Do

Make up a batch of playdough with the children. Let them help you knead it when it has cooled a little. Then add one of the above materials to half the batch and another material to the other half. Try this with lots of materials and find out which textures the children enjoy playing with the most.

AUTUMN-LEAF TREES

Preserve autumn leaves with this simple activity.

What You Need

- Autumn leaves • Clear adhesive plastic • Scissors
- A hole punch • String or thin ribbon
- Large bare branch • Bucket or large tin

What To Do

Next time you are in a park or garden admiring the magnificent autumn foliage, help the children collect a variety of autumn leaves to take home and turn into a beautiful decoration.

Have the children press the autumn leaves between clear pieces of adhesive plastic. Then they should carefully cut around the outside of the leaves leaving a little border. Punch a hole at the top of the leaf and thread some string or ribbon through. Attach the pretty leaves to the bare branch.

Stand the branch in a suitable container and enjoy autumn inside.

BALLOON HEADS

Make a whole family of colourful Balloon Heads for your children to play with. Simple, cheap and lots of fun.

What You Need

- Balloons • Funnel • Plain flour • Water
- Teaspoon • Permanent marking pens

What To Do

Together, blow up the balloons and then deflate them. Put the funnel into each balloon's mouth and carefully spoon in as much flour as you can. Add a little water to make the flour pliable and tie up the balloon.

Your children will love making faces on their balloon heads and moulding them to make funny facial features—big ears, squashed noses and fat cheeks!

BUBBLE PICTURES

Help your children make beautiful bubble pictures.
These colourful paintings make great wrapping paper, too!

What You Need

- Margarine containers • Water • Powder paints
- Liquid detergent • Drinking straws • Paper

What To Do

Half fill each margarine container with water and add some powder paint and a little detergent. Place a drinking straw in each container. Show your children how to blow into the container until it is almost overflowing with bubbles. Press the paper on top of the container and when you take it off there will be beautiful bubble prints on it.

Another method is to place the straw in the bubble mixture and hold a finger over the end to retain some mixture, then your children blow into the straw to blow lots of bubbles over the paper. As the bubbles burst they make colourful bubble prints on the paper.

Make sure that your children understand not to suck the liquid however!

CLAY PINCH POTS

Children will enjoy learning new ways of playing with clay.

What You Need

- Lumps of clay (golf-ball size) • A table or board

What To Do

Show the children how to hold one of the balls of clay in the palm of one hand. Explain that you are going to make a pot. Use your thumb to push a hole in the centre of the clay, but take care not to push your thumb all the way through. Use your palm to support the ball of clay as you turn and push it out with your fingers. You are enlarging the pot by stretching the walls, but it is important to push and turn steadily so the pot sides are even.

This is harder than it sounds and young children will have to practise many times to perfect the technique. If they lose interest, let them just play with the clay and shown them again some other time.

When the pot is round, push the base onto your table or board to make it flat so it will stand.

If your children want to save their pots, leave them in the sun to dry for a few days. Make sure you choose a safe place. Your children might like to paint or decorate their pots, too.

3+

CLIPBOARD CAR ART

*Clipboards are great for the car. Buy one for each child
for long trips and stop the back-seat boredom.*

What You Need

- Clipboards
- Coloured pencils, crayons or felt pens
- Activity books

What To Do

Long car trips are tedious for everyone, but for most families they are inevitable. Children love to draw, colour or work in activity books to help pass the time, but the books are often difficult to balance on their laps in the back of a fast-moving vehicle. Buying a clipboard for each child (in different colours so there are no arguments) overcomes this problem. They simply clip their paper or whatever to the clip at the top of the board and the boards are sturdy enough to support their work. Perhaps the children could draw some of the scenery they observe as you drive along, or make a list of the special things they would like to do on their holiday.

Hint!

Clipboards are terrific for children to draw on when they are sick in bed, or to use for work that the teacher sends home.

COLOUR MIXING

Great fun and your children learn how colours are formed.

What You Need

- Glass jars • Clear plastic containers • Jug of water
- Red, yellow and blue powder paint
- Plastic eye-droppers

What To Do

Help your younger children to half fill the containers and jars with water from the jug. This may be a new skill to learn. Older children will be able to manage it on their own.

Next help your children add some of the red, yellow and blue paint to three of the plastic containers. They then use the eye-droppers to add drops of colour to the jars with the plain water to make lots of new colours.

Arrange the finished jars on a shelf or table with the sun shining through them to make rainbows.

Later the children might like to add a mixture of cornflour and water to the jars and see:

How the colours change
The intensity of the shades
How the clear colours become opaque

COLOURFUL DANCING

*Children love dancing, and some pretty dancing skirts
and floaty wristbands will really enhance their enjoyment.*

What You Need

- Colourful pieces of tulle • Scissors
- Needle and thread • Elastic
- Safety pin • Fabric paint (optional)
- Fabric glue, sequins, diamantes (optional)
- Lengths of satin hair ribbons in different widths and colours
- Small bells (optional)

What To Do

Dancing skirts are easily made by cutting the tulle to the length you need and sewing a casing along the top. Thread elastic through the casing with a safety pin, and sew up the side seam.

If you are really creative you can decorate the skirts with fabric paint, or use fabric glue to stick on some sparkly sequins and diamantes.

To make some floaty wristbands simply tie or sew lengths of different-coloured satin ribbon onto elastic. Tie or sew the elastic to fit your children's wrists. As they dance and wave their arms the ribbons float out and look beautiful. If you want tinkly wristbands sew a few little bells on as well.

CRAZY CORK SNAKES

*Your children will have lots of fun playing with these
fun cork critters—and they're so easy to make!*

What You Need

- Corks (can be purchased at most good craft stores)
- String • Scissors • Very large needle • Newspaper
- Art smocks • Powder paints • Brushes

What To Do

First, cut a piece of string around 60 cm (24 in) long and tie a knot in one end. Thread the large needle onto the string (your needle must be a large heavy one, as it has to pierce all the way through the cork). Thread the corks onto the string, one by one. When you are close to the end of the string, take off the needle and tie a knot in it. Leave a little loose string at the end, on the other side of the knot. Fray it out a little. This is the snake's tongue.

Spread a table with newspapers and dress your children in their art smocks or old shirts. Give them a cork snake each and let them paint the snakes in the colours of their choice. Then put the snakes aside for a few hours and let them dry. Your children will love playing with their crazy cork pets!

DIFFERENT DRUMS

Make a variety of simple homemade drums. Playing simple instruments can help develop a child's sense of rhythm.

What You Need

- Containers such as cardboard cylinders and tins
- A variety of 'skins' for the drums, such as balloons, greaseproof paper, plastic, thin rubber sheeting, wrapping paper • Strong rubber bands • Cord

What To Do

The children will love helping you make and decorate these simple drums. Simply cover a variety of cardboard cylinders and tins with different 'skins'. Use the strong rubber bands to hold the skins on the drums. (To make some of the skins even tighter for higher sounds, you can dip paper in water first and stretch it on wet.)

Show the children how to play the drums by tapping the skin with their fingers.

You can also attach cord to the sides of some of the drums so the children can wear them round their necks and be a marching band. (One of the advantages of these homemade drums is that they are not noisy enough to have the neighbours up in arms!)

FINGER PUPPETS

Make some simple finger puppets with your children,
then settle down with a 'cuppa' to watch the show.

What You Need

- Old gloves (rubber gloves are fine) • Permanent felt pens
- Strong glue • Wool, sequins, small buttons, other decorations
- Shoebox • Scissors

What To Do

Cut off the fingers of a pair of gloves and help your children decorate them to make some finger puppets. Use the felt pens to draw faces or glue on small buttons or sequins for facial features. Make beards with cotton wool, dresses with scraps of fabric, and hair with wool. You'll all have lots of fun thinking of details.

If your children want a puppet theatre for their puppets to perform in, this is easily made from a cereal carton or a shoebox. Stand it on end and then cut a window near the top for the puppets to perform in. Your children will enjoy decorating the puppet theatre, too.

Gather the rest of the family, make some popcorn and sit back to enjoy the show.

FIRST LACING CARDS

This is a good pre-sewing activity and is great for hand-eye coordination.

What You Need

- Thick cardboard • Hole punch
- Lacing materials such as shoelaces

What To Do

Visit your local picture framer for a supply of the thick card they use for picture mounts. Cut the card into simple shapes or even shapes like toys or perhaps fruit. (You are only limited by your imagination and your art ability!)

Now punch holes around the edge of the shapes at least 3 cm (1 in) apart for your children to lace through.

With younger children it is safer not to use a bodkin so you will need threading materials that are stiff enough to thread without one. Old shoelaces are ideal, plastic lacing is cheap to buy by the metre from craft shops or most haberdasheries. You can even dip the ends of wool or string into melted candle wax or a strong laundry starch solution to stiffen them. Make sure you tie the lacing through a hole to start.

FUN WITH CLAY

Clay is one of the easiest art materials for children to use.
Playing with clay provides great exercise for young hands,
and this will help improve pencil grips at school.

What You Need

- Clay • Plastic tablecloth (optional)
- Lino or vinyl work boards about 30 cm (12 in) square (optional)
- Heavy-duty garbage bag with a twist tie
- Old towel • Fishing line

What To Do

Clay is a great material for children. They love the feel of it and the fact they can quickly make great creations. It is very cheap, easily obtainable (from craft shops or your local pottery supply shop) and can be used over and over again.

I put an old plastic tablecloth on our wooden outdoor setting and my son works with his clay on top of it. When he's finished, I simple hose off the tablecloth or throw it in the washing machine. Individual work boards are another alternative.

I keep our clay wrapped in an old damp towel in a plastic garbage bag, tied with a twist tie, and use a short length of fishing line to cut it into small blocks when required.

Special 'works of art' can be saved by leaving them out in the sun to dry for a few days, then they can be painted. However, children are usually content to just model with the clay.

GOOP

Goop is lovely and gooey and fun to play with. You can buy commercial goop, but it is cheap and easy to make your own with the kids.

What You Need

- Two packets of cornflour (made from corn, not wheat)
- Food colouring • Water • Large mixing bowl
- Plastic tablecloth • Container with a lid

What To Do

The children will enjoy helping you make the goop. First, tip the cornflour into a bowl. Add a few drops of food colouring and a little water, until it is the desired consistency.

Spread the tablecloth over a table outside and tip the goop out. The children will have great fun drawing, playing, and feeling the ooey, gooey goop.

When the goop begins to dry out, the children simply add a little more water to make it runny again.

When the children have finished playing, spoon the goop into a plastic container with a lid and store it away. The goop will dry out, but it can be restored to its gooey consistency by simply adding some water.

JUNK THREADING

Children love making their own jewellery!

What You Need

- Bodkins for younger children—tapestry needles for older ones
- Wool or embroidery cotton • Fine hat elastic (for bracelets)
- Shapes cut from coloured cardboard or greeting cards
- Wide variety of threading materials, such as milk bottle tops (punch holes in plastic ones with a hole punch) soft-drink or beer bottle tops (use a hammer and nail to punch the holes)
- Matchboxes • Macaroni • Pieces of lace or other lovely woven fabrics
- Cut up egg cartons (with holes punched in them)
- Cardboard cylinder (cut into short lengths) • Straws
- Dough or clay beads (baked in a slow oven) • Cotton wool
- Patty pans • Paper beads (roll brightly coloured paper strips around a pencil, glue and leave to dry) • Buttons or old beads

What To Do

Thread the bodkin or tapestry needle with wool or cotton and knot near the top. Thread an object on to the wool or cotton and knot at the bottom. Your children then thread on objects to make their jewellery.

Keep all the threading items in takeaway food or margarine containers for easy packing away.

KEY WIND CHIMES

Help the children make a tinkly wind chime from keys. Hang it in the garden so the whole family can enjoy the music of the breeze.

What You Need

- Old keys • Fishing line
- Driftwood or pieces of wood

What To Do

Ask your friends and family for any spare keys they may have. Help the children cut pieces of fishing line and tie them onto each key.

Experiment with hanging the keys from a piece of wood or a piece of driftwood from the beach. The keys need to hang at different heights to balance, but must still be able to hit each other as they swing in the wind. Hang the wind chime from a branch of a tree or under a pergola.

The key wind chime will make a lovely musical sound in your garden as it swings in the breeze.

MAGIC PLAYDOUGH

A fun way to help your children learn how to make new colours.

What You Need

- Playdough (see p46)
- Food colouring or powder paint

What To Do

Make up the playdough recipe with your children, but do not add any food colouring. Divide the playdough into six balls. In the middle of each ball of playdough hide some food colouring or powder paint (make two balls each of red, yellow and blue).

First, give your children a ball with yellow paint hidden in it and one with red. As they play, the colours will appear and then combine to form orange. Magic!

Later, they can combine red and blue to make purple, and blue and yellow to make green. All the balls combined will form brown playdough.

Talk with them about what they have learnt and about the new colours they have made.

MAKE A MOBILE

Young children love watching mobiles swing in the breeze. Help your children make one for their room or as a special gift for a new baby.

What You Need

- Wire coat-hanger or ice-cream container lid
- Bodkin • Wool or embroidery cotton
- Junk for threading (see p73)

What To Do

After your children have made four or five lengths of threading, tie the lengths securely to a wire coat-hanger or through holes punched in an ice-cream container lid. Make sure the mobile is balanced, then hang it on a hook in the ceiling of your children's room.

Mobiles are also great to hang above a baby's change table.

MAKE A PLACEMAT

*Your picky eaters may enjoy meals more when
they eat off their custom-made placemat.*

What You Need

- A piece of thick cardboard cut to the desired size
- Crayons and felt pens • Collage materials
- Scissors • Clear adhesive plastic

What To Do

Have your children decorate their cardboard pieces any way they like. They could decorate them with collage materials, magazine pictures, draw or paint on them or even use dried leaves or flowers from the garden.

They may want to fringe the edges of their cardboard pieces, too. This looks great and provides useful cutting practice for younger children.

When the decorating is finished, cover completely the cardboard pieces with plastic (top and bottom to protect against spills) or have them laminated. (Many photocopying shops or even your children's school or kindergarten have laminators and will do it for a small fee.)

Perhaps your budding artists might like to make a complete set of placemats for the whole family. This might encourage them to help set the table!

MAKE A SOCK PUPPET

Children love making puppets!

What You Need

- Old socks • Buttons • Bits and pieces from your sewing box
- Craft glue • Permanent felt pens • Needle and cotton

What To Do

If your home is like mine, whenever I clean out the drawers (particularly my husband's), there are always quite a few odd socks. It is one of life's little mysteries—where are their mates? Does my washing machine gobble them? Does the dog bury them? Anyway, your children will think it's great fun making them into puppets.

Younger children will need your help to glue on buttons or other bits and pieces to make eyes. Help them mark a mouth with a felt pen, too. Older children will enjoy the challenge of sewing on buttons and other decorations from your sewing box.

Sock puppets are limited only by the creator's imagination, but one of the creatures that children enjoy making out of socks is dinosaurs. Take your children to see the dinosaur exhibits at your local museum or read books about dinosaurs together, and the ideas will just flow.

Making a sock puppet is also a great opportunity to teach your older children how to sew on their own buttons!

PAINT PALETTE

A cheap and easy way to provide paints for your children.

What You Need

- A plastic egg carton or an ice-cube tray
- Powder paints (available at toy shops)
- Water • Fine brushes or cotton buds

What To Do

Watercolour palettes can be quite expensive to buy but you can easily make your own at home.

Put some powder paint into the segments of the egg carton or ice-cube tray and then add a little water to mix. (Hint: make the colours quite strong.) Allow it to dry and harden for a few days.

Give your children some paper and small brushes or cotton buds, and they'll have lots of fun painting with their own homemade palette. Don't forget to give them a jar of clean water too, so they can wash the brushes!

SAND PAINTINGS

Children love the texture of sand, and they will enjoy
the novelty of painting with coloured sand.

What You Need

- Fine beach sand • Large salt shakers or plastic containers without lids
- Powder paints • Glue • Paper or card

What To Do

Put some fine sand into each of the plastic containers or salt shakers. Add a different powder paint colour to each container and mix. Now you have a selection of coloured sand.

Have the children use the glue to 'draw' a picture on paper or card. If younger children find this difficult, have them draw with a pencil first and then glue over their drawing. Next, they sprinkle or shake the coloured sand over their glue picture. When the pictures have dried, display them proudly.

SELF-PORTRAITS

Encourage your children to draw by always having drawing paper, crayons, coloured pencils and felt pens available.

What You Need

- Time together
- Drawing materials
- Paper

What To Do

From an early age children should be encouraged to draw.

Ask your children to draw a self-portrait. Let them look in a mirror for inspiration or talk about the things they like doing best and they can draw themselves doing this. Another idea is to look at photos of themselves and get ideas from these.

Date and name these self-portraits and save them in a special place. You will be surprised when you look back together at how much these self-portraits change over time.

SHOE PRINTS

Children are fascinated by shoe prints. Help your children to compare the shoe patterns on your family's shoes.

What You Need

- A collection of shoes • Plain white paper
- White candle or white crayon
- Food colouring or powdered paint
- Water • Paintbrush

What To Do

Many shoes have interesting textured patterns on the soles. To help your children compare the patterns, turn the shoes upside down and press a sheet of white paper firmly onto the sole of each shoe.

To see the pattern help the children rub a candle or a white crayon over the paper.

Make up some water paint by mixing some food colouring or powdered paint with water. Next, the children use a brush to apply a wash of the water paint to the paper. Then the pattern on the sole of the shoe will be clearly visible.

Put some sheets of paper in front of the door so the family have to walk on them. The kids will have fun playing 'shoe detectives' as they compare and match the patterns left by the different shoes.

SOAP CRAYONS

You can buy commercial soap crayons, but your children will love helping you make some, and they'll love using them, too!

What You Need

- 1 cup soap flakes
- 40 drops strong food colouring
- 2 tablespoons water
- 1 tablespoon cooking oil

What To Do

Mix all the ingredients together making sure there is plenty of colour. Stir really well until you have a thick paste with no lumps.

You can pour the mixture into ice-cube trays to set, but I think it works best if it is simply rolled into thick crayon-like sticks.

Leave the crayons to dry for a few days, then give them to the children. They will love drawing with them on paper, on pavers or concrete, or on the tiles while they are in the bath. The best thing of all is that their drawings can be very easily cleaned off when they have finished.

SOCK SNAKE

Next time you find an odd sock, help your young children make it into a 'sock snake'. They will use it in their imaginative play and it will become a favourite friend.

What You Need

- Scrap paper to tear • Old long sock
- Coloured paper or stickers for the face
- Strong glue

What To Do

Give your children a newspaper or other scrap paper to tear into small pieces for the filling. This is an excellent fine-motor activity to help strengthen their finger muscles.

When they have torn up enough, let them fill their sock (make sure they push the paper right down to the toe).

They might like to use stickers to make a face on their sock snake or cut out pieces of paper to glue on. Stripes or spots of paper add interest also.

Together think of a funny name for the snake—maybe Socks or Snakey!

SPLATTER PAINTINGS

A quick and easy way to decorate paper.

What You Need

- Large sheets of white paper
- Containers of acrylic paint
- One brush per container
- Art smocks

What To Do

Spread out the paper on the grass outside or peg some paper on an easel if you have one.

Show your children how to dip a brush in the paint and flick it with their fingers so the paint flies onto the paper.

Make sure your children wear an art smock or an old shirt over their clothes because this activity is fairly messy.

Splatter paintings make great wrapping paper and they are also good for covering school books.

SPRAY PAINTINGS

Save your old household spray bottles for this fun painting activity.

What You Need

- Spray bottles • Food colouring • Water
- Paper • Pegs • Art smocks

What To Do

This is definitely an outside activity and only to be done on a very still day! Mix up some food colouring and water in the spray bottles (make sure they have been well washed out first).

Peg up some paper on an easel, between two trees, or on the fence. Show the children how to spray with short bursts and encourage them to use lots of different colours to see how the colours mix and make new colours. Discourage your children from spraying too much on each piece of paper—if the paper becomes too wet it will fall to bits.

Spray paintings look sensational and make great wrapping paper.

Hint!

If you don't have an art smock to cover your child's clothes, use an old shirt, done up back-to-front. On hot days let the children spray paint in their swimming costumes—but don't forget the sunscreen.

TWINKLE, TWINKLE

3

Take your children outside at night to look at the stars and teach them the old song 'Twinkle, Twinkle, Little Star'. Next day, try this 'star painting'.

What You Need

- Cardboard for stencils • Scissors
- Black paper • White paint • Paintbrush

What To Do

Carefully cut out some star shapes in different pieces of cardboard. Help each child position the first stencil on their sheet of black paper and paint the inside of the stencil with the white paint. Repeat with different stencils (be careful not to smudge the wet paint!) until each child has a beautiful starry nightscape to hang in their bedroom.

ABORIGINAL RHYTHM STICKS

Australian Aborigines use rhythm sticks in their ceremonial dances and music. Make some simple rhythm sticks with the children so they can keep the beat to their favourite songs.

What You Need

- Lengths of dowel or broom handles
- Ruler • Pencil • Saw • Paints

What To Do

Carefully measure the dowel or broom sticks into equal lengths and then saw off. You may need to sand the ends if they are a little rough.

Show the children some books about Aboriginal art so they can decorate their rhythm sticks authentically.

When the sticks are dry, sing some songs that you all know. Bang your rhythm sticks to the beat.

BLOW PAINTINGS

*Blow paintings are a great way of making attractive wrapping
paper that the children will love giving to their friends!*

What You Need

- Newspaper or sheet of plastic or vinyl tablecloth
- Art smocks • Food colouring or powder paint
- Plastic containers full of water • Drinking straws • Paper

What To Do

Cover an outdoor table with newspaper, a plastic sheet or a vinyl tablecloth as this activity can be
fairly messy. Make sure the children cover their clothes with a smock or an old shirt.

Add some food colouring or powder paint to the water in the containers to make nice strong
primary colours. This activity helps children learn how new colours are made when colours mix.

Place sheets of paper over the covered table. Show the children how to trap some of the water
paint in a straw by putting it in the mixture, putting a finger over the top, then moving the straw
to the paper. The next step is to blow gently over the paper. The paint will spread over the paper
in vein-like formations. As the children use different colours, new colours will form.

BODY CUTOUTS

4

Make outlines of your children's bodies for them to decorate.

What You Need

- Large sheets of paper big enough for your children to lie on
- Felt pen • Scissors • Paints or collage materials

What To Do

Have each child lie on a sheet of paper with their arms and legs out. You then carefully draw around the body to make an outline.

When the outlines are finished, the children may like to cut them out. If your children are still learning to use scissors, you can help them. Some children may prefer to leave their outlines uncut.

Hang the outlines from the fence or Blu-Tack them to a wall outside, and let your children paint and decorate them. Hang the dry outlines on the doors of the children's bedrooms.

Hint!

Your local newspaper office sells the ends of rolls of newsprint very cheaply. A roll will give you years of great drawing paper and is perfect for activities like this.

BOTTLE-TOP TAMBOURINES

Children love percussion instruments and many of them are very easy to make. Make these simple tambourines with the children and start a homemade band.

What You Need

- Offcuts of pine
- Metal bottle tops—beer bottle tops are ideal
- Nails • Hammer

What To Do

The children will love helping you make these simple percussion instruments. Most timber yards or furniture manufacturers will let you have small offcuts of pine. Simply help the children hammer four to six bottle tops into each small piece of pine. Don't hammer the nails in all the way—leave some room for the bottle tops to shake around.

Now the children can shake the wood in time to music, or bang it on their other hand to the beat.

Sing lots of songs you all know with strong beats—nursery rhymes are ideal or songs like 'Frère Jacques'.

CLAY DINOSAUR WORLD

Most children have collections of small dinosaurs. In this activity, children use clay to make a prehistoric land for their dinosaurs to live in.

What You Need

- Books about dinosaurs • Clay
- Blue and red cellophane or a small mirror
- Grass, leaves, twigs, stones • Dinosaur models

What To Do

Look in dinosaur books together so your children gain an understanding of the world the dinosaurs inhabited. Suggest to them that they might like to make a dinosaur world from clay for their toy dinosaurs.

They can use the clay to model mountains, volcanoes and other features of a prehistoric landscape. Help your children add the cellophane to make 'lakes' and 'volcanic flames'. Snippings from the garden make great 'jungles' and, last of all, they can add the dinosaurs.

If your children want to keep their dinosaur world it can be left in the sun to dry, but usually with young children the fun is in the creating and playing. Why don't you take some photos for them to remember their great dinosaur land?

FENCE WEAVING

*Children are fascinated by the way cloth is woven
and will enjoy doing some weaving of their own.*

What You Need

- A scrap of fabric with a loose weave, such as hessian or linen
- Ribbons, lengths of old fabrics, strips of coloured paper
- Chain-wire fence • Scissors • Sheets of paper

What To Do

If you have a chain-wire fence you can decorate it with the children and help them learn about weaving at the same time.

First, show your children a piece of material that has a loose weave, such as hessian or linen. Pull out a thread slowly so they can see the way it has been woven into the fabric.

Now the children can practise weaving on the fence. Give them some ribbons, lengths of old fabrics, or paper strips. The children will enjoy weaving the materials in and out and in and out.

Follow this up by trying some paper weaving with them. Cut several lengths of paper and make some slits in a sheet of paper. They can weave the lengths in and out of the paper going under and over, under and over, for one row, and then over and under, over and under for the next. Eventually the whole sheet of paper will be woven.

GLOVE PUPPETS

Make some simple fabric puppets for your children to decorate.

What You Need

- White cotton fabric (calico is ideal)
- Felt pens • Fabric glue
- Collage items such as sequins, buttons, wool, fabric scraps

What To Do

Have each child place a hand on a doubled-over piece of fabric approximately 20 cm x 15 cm (8 in x 6 in). Draw around the outline of the hand with a felt pen, leaving room for a seam allowance.

Stitch the puppets on your sewing machine. Turn them inside out and press flat with your iron.

Your children will have lots of fun decorating their puppets with sequins, buttons etc. They might make characters out of fairy tales, such as Goldilocks and the Three Bears, or even puppets of family members.

If your children make several puppets, they can have a puppet show. Help them make a puppet theatre out of a large box, then settle down and enjoy the show.

HAMMERING AND NAILING

4+

*Children love using real tools. Teach them how
to use hammers and nails at an early age.*

What You Need

- Soft offcuts of pine • Hammers • Nails of all sizes
- A selection of junk materials such as fabric scraps,
bottle tops, cardboard, paper, patty pans,
pieces of ice-cream container lids

What To Do

I have found in many years of teaching that it is easy to collect soft pine offcuts. Take a large cardboard box to a local cabinetmaker or roof-truss manufacturer and leave it there for a few days. When you call back you will have a box full of lovely pine offcuts for the kids to use.

Buy a selection of nails, but begin with nails that have large heads. The children will need to work on concrete or at a table or bench that's at their height.

It is easiest for them to begin by hammering a selection of junk materials onto a piece of wood, but as they gain mastery over the hammer, they will enjoy joining pieces of wood together.

When they have finished making their creations, they may like to paint them.

4+

MESH WEAVING

Young children love to weave and this simple activity helps them understand how fabric is made.

What You Need

- Plastic mesh—available from hardware stores
- Natural materials such as bark strips, cloth strips, grasses, long leaves, paper strips, string, rope, wool

What To Do

Show the children how to weave in and out of their pieces of mesh with the materials. They will have lots of fun making up interesting patterns and using a variety of materials.

MUSICAL JARS

A simple way to make music together.

What You Need

- Four to six similar empty glass bottles (coffee jars are ideal)
- Metal spoons

What To Do

Leave one bottle empty. Fill the other bottles with varying amounts of water, and fill one completely. Add a little food colouring to the water to make the water level easy to see.

Let your children experiment with the different sounds the bottles make by tapping them with the spoons. Arrange them in order so they can hear the notes go higher and lower.

After they have played for a while, ask them to close their eyes and listen carefully while you tap the bottles. Can they tell you which one is being tapped?

Later, they might like to tap (gently) other household items to hear the sounds they make.

PAPERBARK PICTURES

4+

Gather bark from paperbark trees to make some interesting collage pictures with the children.

What You Need

- Paperbark • Cardboard • PVA glue

What To Do

Paperbark trees derive their name from the layers of bark that peel off the trunks and branches in papery sheets. Their botanical name is Melaleuca, and there are more than 100 different kinds of paperbarks ranging from huge trees to small shrubs.

We have a lemon-scented variety growing in our garden, and many parks in Australia have paperbarks as they are not only decorative but hardy. Many of them grow in swampy areas and can tolerate 'wet feet'. The oil from some melaleucas is used for making tea-tree oil and many medicinal and perfume products.

Gather paperbark from under some melaleucas or carefully peel small sections from different trees if you are allowed to. Take the bark home and spread it out on a table in the backyard with the children.

The children will enjoy gluing the paperbark onto pieces of cardboard to make interesting collages.

PERFUMED PLAYDOUGH

4+

Your children will enjoy playing with sweet-smelling playdough.

What You Need

- Playdough recipe (see p46)
- Essences such as strawberry, lemon, peppermint, vanilla, chocolate
(in the baking section of your supermarket)
- Food colouring

What To Do

Make up a batch of playdough and colour it to match the essence you are going to add—yellow for lemon essence, pink for strawberry, and so on. Add plenty of essence so the smell stays in the playdough.

Give the playdough to your children to play with, but make sure they understand that this is a smelling experience and not a tasting one!

ROSE-COLOURED GLASSES

*Children love looking at the world through
glasses that have different-coloured 'lenses'.*

What You Need

- Cardboard toilet rolls or lunch-wrap cylinders
- Scraps of coloured cellophane • Sticky tape or glue

What To Do

Help your children cover one end of each cardboard cylinder with a scrap of coloured cellophane. Now they have coloured telescopes. They can look through them to see a different-coloured world!

They can also cut the middle out of a paper plate and replace it with cellophane to make a good 'view finder'. Another suggestion is take the lenses out of old sunglasses or reading glasses and make coloured lenses out of cellophane.

SAWDUST MODELLING

4+

Make an interesting modelling mixture for the children from sawdust and glue.

What You Need

- Sawdust (from your local sawmill, timber yard or hardware store)
- Wallpaper paste • Large bowl • Water • Drinking straws
- Toothpicks • Pipe-cleaners • Acrylic paints

What To Do

This is a messy activity and is best done outside.

Mix two cups of the sawdust to one cup of wallpaper paste in a bowl, and slowly add enough water to form a modelling dough.

The children will love making the dough into interesting shapes and figures. They can use the straws, toothpicks and pipe-cleaners to add interesting features. They might like to model jungle animals, dinosaurs, aliens or anything else they can imagine.

Leave the models in the sun until they are dry, then the children can enjoy painting them.

SIMPLE GUITAR

Help your children make a very simple guitar out of an old shoebox.
It won't make the lovely sounds of a real guitar, but your
children will enjoy strumming it just as much.

What You Need

- Shoebox with a lid • Scissors
  - Six to eight thick rubber
  bands of different sizes

What To Do

Cut a hole in the lid of the shoebox about 8 cm (3 in) in diameter. Put the lid back on the shoebox and press down hard on the lid so the rubber bands won't actually touch it and deaden the sound.

Now stretch the rubber bands right around the box and position over the sound hole.

As your children pluck the rubber bands they will hear the different sounds.

STOCKING BABY

*With a little help your children can make their
own 'stocking babies' to love and cuddle.*

What You Need

- Pantihose • Scissors
- Filling such as cushion filling,
  cotton wool, old fabrics
- Needle and cotton
- Rubber bands
- Buttons • Felt pen • Wool

What To Do

Cut off the lower part of the pantihose below the knees. Stuff with filling to make the baby's arms, then sew shut the openings.

Stuff and then knot the original thigh part of the pantihose to form the baby's feet. Fill the section of pantihose above this with stuffing. Sew or knot the waistband to make the top of the baby's head. Twist a rubber band below its head to make its neck and, lastly, sew the arms onto the body.

Your children can help you make their baby's face. Buttons look great or perhaps embroider or draw on a mouth. Wool can be sewn on for its hair.

Your children might like to dress their baby in some of their own tiny baby clothes.

THE DINGLE DANGLE SCARECROW

Sing this funny song with your children (they will know it from kindergarten or pre-school) as you help them make a scarecrow for the garden.

What You Need

- Pantihose • Rags or more old pantihose for stuffing
- Needle and strong thread • Permanent pens
- Old hat • PVA glue • Old clothes
- A strong garden stake or broom handle • Hay

What To Do

Begin by stuffing the top of a pair of pantihose with rags or more pantihose for the head. Sew up the top with strong thread. The children will enjoy drawing on the scarecrow's facial features with permanent pens. Use the glue to attach some straw to his hat and place it on his head.

Next fill the legs of the pantihose and tie together to form the body. Tie on two more legs for arms. Stuff another pair of pantihose to make the bottom and legs, and sew on to the body. Dress the scarecrow in some old clothes—an old shirt and pair of pants are ideal. Stuff some straw into the arms of the shirt and legs of the pants for his hands and feet.

Find a spot in the garden for your scarecrow and attach it to a well-anchored stake or broom handle.

FOOD FUN

CHOCCY BANANA ICEBLOCKS

Children love bananas and they are very good for them.
When you have a lot to use up, try this delicious recipe.

What You Need

- Bananas • Cooking chocolate • Knife
- Ice-cream sticks • Tray

What To Do

Your children can help by peeling the bananas, and the older ones can cut the bananas in half (across). Poke an ice-cream stick into the end of each banana, then place them on a tray and freeze. When they are frozen, dip them in the melted chocolate. Very yummy!

EGG FLIP

Whenever my child is off his food, an egg flip is something I can always get into him. What's more, he likes to help me make it!

What You Need

- 1 egg • Vanilla essence • 1 cup milk
- 2 teaspoons sugar • Nutmeg
- Banana (optional) • Mixing bowl
- Wooden spoon • Glass

What To Do

Your children can help you collect all the ingredients and utensils, then ask one of them to break the egg into the bowl. Next, add some vanilla and the sugar. Hold the bowl while the children take it in turns beating the mixture until it is frothy. Next, pour in one cup of milk and add a banana (optional), then beat it again.

Pour the egg flip into a glass and sprinkle the top with a little nutmeg. This makes one drink. To make more, multiply the ingredients by the number of children.

FRENCH TOAST

A yummy breakfast that is easy to cook together.

What You Need

- 1 egg • $\frac{1}{2}$ cup milk • 2 teaspoons butter • 4 slices of bread
- Honey, golden syrup or maple syrup • Mixing bowl
- Wooden spoon • Frypan

What To Do

Help your child crack the egg into a bowl and beat it, then add the milk. Mix well. Melt the butter in a frypan and, when it is bubbling, dip two slices of bread in the egg mixture and cook. Turn once.

Serve warm with honey, golden syrup or maple syrup. We like it with maple syrup in our house—it's our favourite Sunday morning breakfast.

FROG IN A POND

An old family favourite that is perfect for parties or as a special after-dinner treat.

What You Need

- Packet of green jelly • Boiling water
- Chocolate frogs • Chocolate buttons
- Large, shallow bowls

What To Do

Mix up the jelly according to the instructions on the packet. Then pour it into the individual bowls. Allow to cool and then stand in the fridge.

Once the jelly is completely set, the children can decorate their bowls with chocolate frogs and add chocolate buttons for water lilies. It's best to give each child a set number of frogs and buttons so that they don't go overboard and end up with more chocolate than jelly in their bowls!

If making frog in a pond for dessert, it's a good idea to have your children decorate their frogs a couple of hours earlier and return their bowls to the fridge. Then sit back and watch reluctant eaters eat their main course at a great rate, knowing their delicious dessert is waiting for them!

JUNKET

Junket is a yummy, healthy dessert that your young children will enjoy helping you make. We always loved it as children—try it with your own kids.

What You Need

- 1 junket tablet (sold in packets in your supermarket)
- 1 teaspoon water • 1½ cups milk • 2 teaspoons sugar
- Food colouring • Nutmeg, coconut or sprinkles
- Saucepan • Wooden spoon

What To Do

Your children will enjoy watching the junket tablet dissolve in a teaspoon of water. Meanwhile, heat the milk in a saucepan, but only until blood heat—the junket will not set if the milk is too hot. Stir the dissolved tablet into the milk. Your children can add a few drops of food colouring if they like. Pour the junket into serving bowls. Adults like nutmeg or coconut sprinkled on the top, but my bet is the children will want colourful sprinkles on theirs.

Chill the junket in the fridge for a few hours before serving. Makes four servings.

BANANA PANCAKES

Nutritionists tell us that we should eat a banana a day. When you have some extra-ripe bananas in the house, help your children make some banana pancakes for a health snack.

What You Need

- 2 ripe bananas • 1 egg • 1 cup self-raising flour
- ³/₄ cup milk • 1 teaspoon butter • Wooden spoon
- Mixing bowl • Whisk • Tea towel • Frypan • Egg lifter

What To Do

Let the children help you mash the bananas well. Ask one of them to break the egg and whisk well into the bananas, until smooth and creamy. Next, measure in the flour and half of the milk and beat for one minute with a large spoon. Stir in the rest of the milk. Cover the mixture with a tea towel and allow it to stand for about half an hour.

Add a teaspoon of butter to a frypan and pour or ladle in some of the mixture to form small pancakes. When bubbles appear on the side turn carefully with an egg lifter and cook until golden brown on the other side. Banana pancakes are delicious served warm (with ice cream and sliced bananas) for dessert or served cold for a snack. Makes about twelve.

BUTTERFLY SANDWICHES

*Even the pickiest eaters in your family will love these
sandwiches, especially if they helped in the making.*

What You Need

• Bread • Spreads such as cream cheese,
cheese, peanut paste, vegemite
• Decorations such as cheese slices,
fruit or vegetable pieces, gherkins,
slices of meat, sultanas • Knives • Plates

What To Do

Stand your children on chairs beside you at the kitchen bench so they can help. Cut their slices of bread into either two or four triangles and face them outwards on plates to form the 'butterflies'. Apply a spread to the triangles, then decorate—your children will love helping with this part and making suggestions. Cheese slices cut up with celery pieces are yummy on vegemite, or banana rings and sultanas on peanut paste are just great. Use strips of carrot or capsicum for antennae. Yum! Yum!

CHEERIO KEBABS

Cheerios are also called cocktail sausages. Children love them, though, like most parents, I consider them party fare. However, your children will enjoy helping you make them into exciting kebabs for their own dinner or for a special occasion, such as a birthday party or a sausage sizzle.

What You Need

- 1 kg (2lb) cheerios
- Cherry tomatoes
- Cucumber
- Large can of pineapple pieces
- Can of baby corn cobs
- Stuffed olives (optional)
- Knives
- Bowls
- Kebab sticks or skewers

Marinade:
- Reserved pineapple syrup
- 1 tablespoon brown sugar
- 2 teaspoons french mustard
- 1 tablespoon lemon juice
- Saucepan
- Pastry brush

What To Do

Make the marinade by combining the pineapple syrup, brown sugar, mustard and lemon juice in a saucepan. Bring the mixture to the boil, and boil until it is reduced to a third.

The children can help by dicing the cucumber, cutting the cheerios in half and putting the other ingredients into bowls. Then they will have lots of fun threading their own kebab sticks. (If you soak the wooden skewers or kebab sticks overnight they will be less likely to burn on the grill or barbecue.) Use a pastry brush to brush their finished kebabs with the marinade mixture, and baste them some more while they're cooking. Yum! Any that are left are delicious cold in your children's lunch boxes.

2+

CHOCOLATE CRACKLES

A yummy treat to make with your children for special occasions.

What You Need

- 1¹/₂ cups icing sugar • 4 cups Rice Bubbles
- 3 tablespoons cocoa • 1 cup coconut
- 250 g (8 oz) copha • Flour sifter • Large mixing bowl
- Wooden spoon • Saucepan • Spoons • Tray

What To Do

Your children will enjoy sifting the icing sugar into a large mixing bowl. Next they can measure and add the other dry ingredients. They should mix these well. Meanwhile, melt the copha gently in a saucepan and cool a little. Carefully pour the copha into the bowl of dry ingredients and mix. Make sure the children are safely away as you do this. When the mixture has cooled enough to handle they will love spooning it into patty pans. Cool on a tray in the refrigerator and enjoy!

EGG CLOWNS

Your children will love helping you make these egg 'clowns'.

What You Need

- Boiled eggs • Tomato sauce
- Salmon with lemon juice or mayonnaise
- Tomato or capsicum slices
- Shredded lettuce • Knife • Plates

What To Do

Show your children how to do the following with their boiled eggs.

First, cut off the top of the egg and place it on the side of the plate to use later. Carefully scoop out the yolk and mix it with a little tomato sauce or perhaps some salmon with lemon juice or mayonnaise. Pile the filling back into the egg and place the top back on to make the clown's hat. Use tiny pieces of tomato or capsicum to make the face. Sit the clown on some shredded lettuce 'grass'. Enjoy!

FIZZY SPIDERS

I don't know why these sweet fizzy drinks are called spiders,
but they're great fun to make and children love them.

What You Need

- Lemonade or other fizzy soft drink
- Ice cream • Spoons
- Tall glasses or plastic cups

What To Do

Give your children a spoon and a glass or plastic cup. Then half fill the glasses or cups with lemonade.

Let each child take a scoop of ice cream out of the tub and drop it into their glass. They must stir the ice cream into the lemonade quickly. Then the drink will froth and foam right up, which the children love.

Experiment with different-coloured soft drinks and ice cream. A great treat for a hot summer's day!

FRUIT KEBABS

*Make eating fruit an exciting experience for your children
by showing them how to thread fruit kebabs.*

What You Need

- A selection of fruits in season, such as apples,
  bananas, kiwi fruit, mandarins, melons,
  oranges, strawberries • Large platter
  • Kebab sticks or skewers • Knife

What To Do

Let your children help you cut the fruit into chunks and slices that will fit on the kebab sticks. Put the fruit on a large platter, provide the children with kebab sticks, and let them thread on their own selection. Make sure they eat the fruit from the side of the sticks so they don't spike their mouths. Children love the novelty of this and even those who are not keen on fruit will enjoy it prepared this way.

2+

FRUIT SMOOTHIES

A great way to get fruit and milk into reluctant eaters.

What You Need

- $\frac{1}{2}$ cup cold full-cream milk
- 6 strawberries or 1 banana
(or any other fruit that will blend well)
- $\frac{1}{4}$ cup flavoured yoghurt
- Blender • Glass

What To Do

Your children will enjoy helping you add all the ingredients to the blender. Blend well until nice and frothy. Pour into a tall glass, add a straw and watch it disappear! Makes enough for one serve.

FUNNY EGG FACES

Sometimes we have to resort to trickery to encourage our children to eat healthy food. Your children will love to help you make these funny egg faces, and will enjoy eating them at the end.

What You Need

- Boiled eggs • Grated cheese, carrot or shredded lettuce
- Sultanas, pieces of tomato or beetroot
- Mayonnaise or cream cheese
- Buttered bread • Knife • Plates

What To Do

Help your children cut their eggs in half and place the halves on their plates. They then use other foods to make hair and facial features on their eggs. Suggest they make a body with triangles or rectangles of buttered bread. Then they get to eat their creations!

2+ GEOMETRIC SANDWICHES

Here's a yummy way to teach your children their shapes!

What You Need

- Sliced bread • Fillings such as avocado, cheese slices, egg, ham, lettuce, peanut paste, sprouts, sultanas, tomato
- Knife • Scone cutter

What To Do

Your children will enjoy helping make the sandwiches. This is a great opportunity to introduce them to new combinations and taste sensations, such as peanut paste and sultanas, or avocado and sprouts.

After the sandwiches are made, help the children to carefully cut them into different shapes—triangles, rectangles and squares. Use a scone cutter to make circles.

Take the sandwiches outside with a large jug of juice. Put a rug in the garden and enjoy a shape picnic together.

MARSHMALLOW DELIGHTS

This is a simple treat that toddlers can help prepare.

What You Need

- Marshmallows
- Jelly crystals
- Sandwich bag

What To Do

Pour a packet of jelly crystals into a clear sandwich bag. Help your toddler drop some marshmallows into the bag, then seal the bag.

Show your toddler how to shake the bag.

The jelly crystals will stick to the marshmallows, making a sweet treat.

PICNIC SANDWICHES

As a pre-school teacher and now as a mother, I have discovered something about children and food. If you involve children in the preparation of the food, they are more likely to eat it. It is not always possible or practical in our busy lives, but try it and see if I am right!

What You Need

- Sliced bread • Butter or margarine
- Sandwich fillings such as avocado, beetroot, chicken, egg, ham, lettuce, sprouts, tomato
- Cutting board • Butter knives • Plates

What To Do

Next time you go on a family picnic take along the sandwich fillings, a couple of types of yummy bread and the butter. Spread the food out on the picnic rug with a big board, plates and spreading knives, and let the children concoct their own delicious sandwiches. They will taste better because they are nice and fresh, and the children will not complain about the fillings when they have made them! In addition, you are developing their independence by showing them they are old enough to do some things for themselves!

ALPHABET BIKKIES

Help your young children learn their letters by making some alphabet bikkies together.

What You Need

- 1 cup self-raising flour • $1/2$ tablespoon cornflour
- $1/3$ cup butter or margarine • $1/4$ cup castor sugar
- 1 beaten egg • Flour sifter • Mixing bowl
- Small bowl • Whisk or fork • Breadboard

What To Do

Help your children sift the flour and cornflour into a mixing bowl. Next, show them how to rub in the butter, then break the egg into a small bowl and beat it with a whisk or fork. Add the egg and sugar to the mixture. Next, lightly flour a board and knead the dough until it's pliable.

Break the dough into small pieces and the children can roll it into little sausages. Help them shape the dough sausages into letters.

Bake the letters at 180°C (350 F) for about twenty minutes and cool on a rack. They are delicious plain or you might like to help the children ice them when they have cooled. Ours never last long enough to be iced! Makes about twelve.

BUTTER CHURNS

Show your children how butter was made in the olden days with this simple butter churn.

What You Need

- 250 ml pure whipping cream
- Jar or plastic container with a secure lid
- One marble

What To Do

Pour the cream into the container and add the marble. Take turns with the children to shake the container (not too hard!). After about ten minutes the cream should have changed into butter (you'll also have some left-over buttermilk to taste).

Compare the butter you have made with commercially made butter you have in the fridge. Can the children see and taste the difference? Explain how butter was traditionally made into small pats and often printed with a simple design.

Make some bread-and-butter sandwiches with the butter you have made together.

FAIRY BREAD

3+

This simple treat is a perennial favourite with children (and many adults!).

What You Need

- Slices of white bread • Margarine or butter
- Coloured sprinkles • Butter knife • Plate

What To Do

Let your children help you spread the slices of bread with butter. Then comes the fun part—the children cover the bread with sprinkles.

Cut the bread into quarters and serve with a cold drink.

Fairy bread is a delicious treat that's great for tea parties in the garden.

GINGERBREAD MEN

Read or tell the story of the Gingerbread Man to your children, and then suggest you make some gingerbread together.

What You Need

- ¹/₂ cup sugar • 125 g (4 oz) butter • 1 egg • 1 cup plain flour
- ¹/₂ teaspoon baking soda • 2 teaspoons ground ginger
- Mixed fruit for decoration • Mixing bowl • Wooden spoon
- Flour sifter • Rolling pin • Floured board • Sharp knife
- Egg lifter • Greased oven tray

What To Do

Cream the sugar and butter, then add the egg and beat well. Let the children use the flour sifter to sift the flour, and then add the baking soda and ginger.

Using a floured rolling pin, roll out the gingerbread on a floured board. The children can help cut out their gingerbread men, and then help lift them with an egg lifter onto a greased oven tray.

Now for the fun stuff! Give the children mixed fruit or even chocolate bits to decorate their gingerbread men. Perhaps they can make a cherry nose, sultana eyes, a peel mouth, and currant or chocolate buttons.

Cook the gingerbread men at 180°C (350 F) for fifteen to twenty minutes.

HOMEMADE LEMONADE

A delicious, refreshing drink your children will enjoy making and sharing with you.

What You Need

- 4 lemons • $1/2$ cup sugar or honey • $1/2$ cup hot water
- 4 cups cold water • Ice cubes • Lemon squeezer
- Large jug • Knife • Juicer • Large jug
- Small jug • Wooden spoon

What To Do

Ask your children to count out four lemons. Help them cut the lemons in half and juice them with a juicer. Pour the juice into a large jug.

Your children can measure out the honey or sugar in a small jug, but add the hot water to dissolve it yourself.

Next, your children add four cups of cold water to the large jug. Add the honey or sugar solution and let them stir it well. Add some lemon slices and ice cubes to the lemonade for a decorative touch.

For a slightly fizzy lemonade you can substitute a bottle of sparkling mineral water or soda water for the plain cold water.

3+ HONEY AND ORANGE WHIP

Make a refreshing and healthy drink for the whole family to enjoy on a hot day.
This drink is also delicious poured into iceblock containers and frozen.

What You Need

- 1 dozen oranges, or a bottle of commercial orange juice and 3 oranges
  - ¼ cup honey • Knife • Juicer • Large jug • Blender

What To Do

Cut the oranges and help your children squeeze them in a juicer. My son loves using our electric juicer to make orange juice for breakfast. Put the juice in a large jug. Next peel the oranges and help the children cut the oranges into segments, making sure you remove all the pips. Combine the orange juice, orange flesh and honey, and blend until smooth. (You'll need to do it in batches.)

This recipe makes about ten cups. Drink some now and pour some into iceblock containers and freeze for a delicious icy treat. Don't forget the ice-cream sticks!

NAME SANDWICHES

Make 'name sandwiches' with your children. It's a fun way of teaching them how to spell their names.

What You Need

- Sliced bread • Butter or margarine
- A favourite spread, such as honey, jam, peanut paste
- Alphabet cereal • Butter knives • Bowl • Plates

What To Do

Apply your children's favourite spread to slices of bread and butter. Pour some of the alphabet cereal into a bowl and help each child find the letters of their name. Write their name with the cereal letters on their slice of bread.

PARFAITS

The whole family will love assembling (and eating) their delicious parfait desserts. They are traditionally made in tall parfait glasses, but any long glasses will be fine. However, you will need spoons with long handles to reach all the delicious dessert at the bottom!

What You Need

- Chopped fruit—tinned or fresh • Jelly
- Custard • Whipped cream
- Crushed nuts and wafer biscuits
- Tall glasses • Serving spoons

What To Do

Let the children help you prepare the fruit, jelly and custard. Set out the glasses and the fillings and let the family layer their own parfaits. They look great with contrasting layers of colour. Top with some toasted or crushed nuts and wafer triangles. They'll be coming back for more!

PICNIC DAMPER

Children love damper, and a barbecue or picnic is not complete without it.
Best of all, your children will love helping to make it.

What You Need

- 3 cups self-raising flour • 1 teaspoon salt
- 1 tablespoon cooking oil • 1½ cups milk
- Extra flour • Large mixing bowl • Floured board
- Greased tin or aluminium foil

What To Do

Let the children help measure all the ingredients. Mix the dry ingredients in a large bowl. Form a well in the centre. Add most of the milk and combine to form a soft, moist dough.

Tip out the damper onto a floured board, and with floured hands knead for a few minutes. Place the damper dough in a greased tin or wrap carefully in aluminium foil. Place in a hot barbecue or in the coals of an open fire.

The damper will take about thirty to forty minutes to cook. Test to see if it is cooked by tapping the base with your knuckles. It should sound hollow when cooked.

Damper is delicious served with golden syrup or honey for dessert, or with plain butter or garlic butter.

PIZZA

A guaranteed culinary success with all the family.

What You Need

- Pita bread or pizza bases • Tomato paste or pizza paste
- Cheese • Bacon • Mild salami sausage
- Vegetables such as zucchini, capsicum, mushrooms, onion and pineapple • Baking tray
- Knife • Cheese grater

What To Do

Place the pizza base on a baking tray and your children can spread the tomato paste over it. Next, they grate the cheese and sprinkle that over the tomato paste.

Together, cut up the bacon, salami and vegetables and sprinkle over the cheese.

Cook in a hot oven for fifteen to twenty minutes.

SHAKE-UP THE MILO

3+

Help your children learn how to make a yummy milk shake.

What You Need

- Milo • Hot water • Milk • Ice cream
- Teaspoon • Glass • Plastic beaker with lid

What To Do

Have your children measure two teaspoons of Milo into the beaker. Add a little hot water yourself, but let them mix it well to dissolve the Milo.

Next, they pour out a glass of milk and add that to the beaker with a big spoonful of ice cream. Help them put the lid firmly on the beaker and they can shake it vigorously.

Let them pour it into a glass and enjoy!

BANANA DATE SQUARES

A healthy snack your children will love helping you make,
and all the family will love eating!

What You Need

- 1 cup dates • $^1/_2$ cup pecan nuts • 3 bananas
- $^1/_3$ cup cooking oil • 1 teaspoon vanilla essence
- 2 cups rolled oats • $^1/_2$ teaspoon salt • Knife
- Mixing bowl • Wooden spoon • Greased baking tray

What To Do

Let older children chop the dates and pecans. Younger children can peel and mash the bananas in the bowl. Add the chopped dates, nuts and oil to the bowl and mix well. Add the vanilla, rolled oats and salt, and again mix well. Let the mixture stand for five minutes so the oats absorb the moisture.

Push into a greased baking tray and bake for twenty-five minutes at 180° C (350 F). Cut into squares while still warm. Yummy, but still healthy.

CHEESE TASTING

It's good to help young children enjoy a wide variety of taste experiences from a very young age. Cheese is an excellent food for growing youngsters, so why not expand their horizons by teaching them a little about different cheese flavours?

What You Need

- Several different cheeses, such as processed cheddar, mild cheddar, tasty cheddar, cottage cheese, Romano cheese, cream cheese • Glasses of water
- Pencil • Paper

What To Do

Out of sight of your children, cut up some small squares of different types of cheese.

Help your children to draw a 'yummy' scale on a large piece of paper. Place each child's name along the top of the paper. Then create a scale down the side of the paper. The categories could be: extra-yummy, yummy, okay, yucky, very yucky!

Give each of your children a small block of cheese to try. Ask them to write down the cheese type on the chart beneath their name, and rate it by ticking one category. Then let them have a drink of water if they want, to wash the taste out of their mouth. Try another piece of cheese. Continue on until they have tried all the cheeses and filled in the chart.

Your children will enjoy sampling the different tastes and learning that not all cheeses taste the same.

DOUGH SCULPTURES

Make delicious dough creations that you and your children can eat. Yum! Yum!

What You Need

- 300 ml warm water • 1 packet yeast
- 1 teaspoon salt • 1 tablespoon sugar
- 4 cups plain flour • 1 egg (beaten)
- Mixing bowl • Wooden spoon
- Greased baking tray
- Tea towel • Pastry brush

What To Do

Help your children pour the warm water into a large bowl. They can then sprinkle on the yeast and stir it until it is soft. Next, they can add the salt, sugar and flour. Mix into a dough.

Show your children how to knead the dough until it is smooth and pliable. They can then shape the dough into whatever takes their fancy e.g. letters, shapes, animals. Put the dough shapes onto a greased baking tray and cover with a tea towel. Leave in a warm spot until they have risen to double in size.

Next, your children can 'paint' their shapes with the beaten egg. Bake the shapes at 180°C (350 F) for ten to fifteen minutes until golden brown.

HEALTHY APRICOT TREATS

A yummy and easy recipe that makes a healthy treat.

What You Need

- 1 cup chopped dried apricots
- $^{1}/_{2}$ cup orange juice • 4 tablespoons honey
- 1 cup powdered milk
- $^{1}/_{2}$ cup desiccated coconut
- Saucepan • Mixing bowl
- Wooden spoon

What To Do

Simmer the apricots, orange juice and honey in a saucepan for about ten minutes. Add the powdered milk. Pour into a mixing bowl and mix well. Chill in the fridge until cool.

Later your children will enjoy rolling the mixture into balls and coating them with coconut.

Store in the fridge, but they won't last long (they're too tasty!). Makes about twenty-four.

JELLY ORANGES

*This delicious jelly treat was a favourite with my sister and me
on hot summer afternoons. It makes a fabulous party dish, too.*

What You Need

- 8 thick-skinned oranges • 2 packets of different-coloured jelly
- Boiling water • Sharp knife • Container • Tray
- Mixing bowls • Wooden spoon

What To Do

First, thoroughly wash the oranges in warm water. Cut the oranges in half and then, using a small sharp knife, cut out the flesh of the oranges and place it in a container (this can be used to make a delicious fruit salad later, or your children might enjoy eating it right away). Your children can help arrange the empty orange halves carefully on a tray, ready to be filled with jelly.

Have the children pour each packet of jelly crystals into a different bowl. Then mix up the jelly according to directions. It sometimes helps to add a little less water than stated on the packet, just to make the jelly set harder in the orange skins.

Pour the jelly into the empty orange halves and place them in the fridge to set. A few hours later, the delicious jelly oranges will be ready to eat!

PIKELET LETTERS

Cooking with children involves many learning areas—reading recipes together, following directions and measuring. As well, making letter pikelets helps them learn the alphabet in a really fun way!

What You Need

- A basic pikelet recipe • Large jug
- Greased pan • Egg lifter

What To Do

Don't forget to involve your children in making the mixture—children always eat more if they have helped in the cooking process.

Make your pikelet batter in a jug for easy pouring. Carefully pour the batter into a hot greased pan. As you pour, make individual letters with the batter. Once the letters begin to bubble you can pour a little more batter onto the top of the letter to form traditional round pikelets and the letter section will stand out in relief when you turn it.

Otherwise just leave the letter shapes and turn them carefully. Your children will have great fun making words from the pikelets, and even more fun eating them!

4+

SANDWICH SMORGASBORD

This idea came from the dental therapists in the School Dental Unit attached to the school where I teach. They organise a wonderful 'Taste Testing for Pre-schoolers' where the children are encouraged to try new, healthy taste sensations. As a mother I find it very disheartening when my child refuses to try new foods. However, I have found that if he is involved in the food preparation he is more likely to try something different.

What You Need

- Breads such as cruskits, foccacia, pita bread, wholemeal bread • Fillings such as alfalfa sprouts, beetroot, carrot, cheese, lettuce, meats, salmon
- Spreads such as avocado, cream cheese, ricotta cheese, hommos, peanut paste, vegemite

What To Do

Let the children help prepare the food. When it is ready, set it out attractively with jugs of cold water and juice, and cups and plates. The children then make exotic sandwiches. Encourage them to try new combinations. After they have finished they might like to draw what they had and make it into a recipe book for future 'sandwich smorgasbords'. Talk about what worked well together and what was 'yucky'.

SOUP FOR LUNCH

Most children love soup, and they will love this tasty, healthy soup even more because they have helped to make it. Bon appétit!

What You Need

- Vegetables such as beans, carrot, celery, parsnip, peas, potato, tomato, zucchini
- Bacon or ham pieces • Olive oil • Stock cube • Dry pasta
- Vegetable peeler • Vegetable knife • Large soup pot

What To Do

Involve your children as much as possible in preparing the soup, letting them peel the potato, scrape the carrot with the vegie peeler, shell the peas and so on.

Cook the bacon or ham in a little oil in a large soup pot. Let your children tip in the prepared vegetables—carefully! Add some water, the stock cube and about half a cup of pasta. Bring the soup to the boil and then let it simmer for about thirty minutes.

This soup tastes delicious served with crusty bread or toast fingers. Your children will enjoy the accolades of the whole family! Makes enough for six.

STICKY JAM TARTS

Children love helping to make these simple jam tarts—and the whole family will love eating them.

What You Need

- Baking spray • Sheets of pre-made sweet shortcrust pastry
- Flour • Jam • Muffin trays or tart trays • Cutting board
- Large circular scone cutter • Teaspoons

What To Do

First, lightly spray the muffin or tart trays with baking spray. Lay out one or two sheets of pastry on a floured board. Then help your children to press the scone cutters into the pastry and cut out as many circles as you have spaces for in the trays. If you don't have a scone cutter, I've found a large cup or mug works just as well as a cutter. Your children can now place each little circle of pastry into the trays. Press each pastry circle gently down into the trays.

Give each child a teaspoon and help them to place one teaspoon of jam into each pastry case. Pop the trays into a medium oven for approximately ten minutes. Keep a close eye on the tarts as they are cooking. When the pastry starts to brown and the jam has spread out and is bubbling, they are ready. Yum!

Important!

When you take the tarts out of the oven, do not let the children touch them until they have cooled. Boiling jam can cause a nasty burn.

VEGETABLE TASTING

*Cooking together can help picky eaters develop an interest
in food and encourages them to try something new.*

What You Need

- Selection of raw vegetables • Vegetable peeler
- Sharp knife • Bowl of cold water • Cutting board

What To Do

Many parents complain that their young children won't eat vegetables, but I have always found at pre-school that they prefer raw vegies to cooked ones. Involve your young children in the preparation of a raw vegetable platter and I'm sure you will be surprised!

Put your children up beside you and they can help wash the vegetables, peel cucumbers and carrots, and help break up vegetables such as cauliflower or broccoli. Older children can use a small sharp knife, but always supervise carefully.

Vegetables can taste delicious on their own, but many children love to dip them in a sauce. Popular sauces and dips include avocado dip, tomato sauce, mild soy sauce, mild sweet-and-sour sauce, or a packet of French onion soup mixed with sour cream or yoghurt. Your child will be able to help make up these simple sauces, too.

Next time your children have friends to play, help them make up a vegie platter and dipping sauce before the friends arrive. You'll be amazed how quickly the food disappears.

WORD PLAY

LIBRARY VISITS

*One of the best ways of getting value for the rates we all pay
to our local councils is to regularly use your local library.*

What You Need

- Time • A local council library
- Proof of residence is required by most libraries

What To Do

Visit the library with your children. If you are not already members take along some proof of address. Children model their reading behaviour on their parents and many studies have shown that children who don't have parents who read often don't see any purpose in learning to read at school. So if you are not a 'reader', try to cultivate the habit or you might find your children aren't interested in books.

Help your children choose their books, making sure they suit their ages and interests. (It's also great to borrow magazines, periodicals and other resources from libraries.) As children become used to the library they will be able to select their own books and, of course, will love having Mum or Dad read to them at home.

Libraries are also a great source of holiday activities. Our local library has story-telling sessions, craft periods and sessions to help children use the library and learn basic computer skills.

ROUND AND ROUND THE GARDEN

Children are never too young to be introduced to rhyme.

What You Need

- Time

What To Do

Rhymes are a great way to help children learn language. Do the finger actions while reciting this rhyme:

Round and round the garden (Run a finger around your child's palm.)
Went the teddy bear.
One step, two steps (Walk your fingers up your child's arm.)
Tickle you under there. (Tickle your child under one arm.)

Round and round the haystack (Repeat actions above.)
Went the little mouse.
One step, two steps
In his little house.

SINGING IN THE CAR

Use trips in the car as an opportunity to sing together and to teach your children new songs. Even if you can't sing in tune, the kids will still love singing with you.

What You Need

- Time in the car

What To Do

When we were children we loved singing in the car with Mum and Dad, and I still sing many of those old songs with my son.

Singing is great for developing a child's language skills, memory and sense of rhythm. Begin with simple nursery rhymes, then progress to the songs your child is learning at kindergarten, pre-school or school. If you don't know the words, why not ask the teacher to write them down for you. Teachers are happy to do this because they value parental interest and support.

If you still need more songs to sing, have a look at the selection of tapes or CDs in your local children's bookshop.

WHERE'S YOUR NOSE?

Start teaching your children the parts of the body from an early age.

What You Need

- Time

What To Do

Every day, touch and name different parts of your child's body. Begin with the head—nose, ear, mouth, teeth, eye (be careful!), chin, cheek and hair. Then touch and name other parts of the body—hand, fingers, foot, toes, leg, arm, stomach, and so on.

You'll be amazed how quickly your child learns the words. Soon, you'll be able to ask your child, 'Where's your nose (or mouth, fingers, arm etc.)?' and she'll respond by touching her nose (or mouth, fingers, arm etc.).

Give your child lots of praise when she gets it right!

BAA, BAA, BLACK SHEEP

Teaching young children lots of nursery rhymes
helps improve their language and memory skills.

What You Need

- Time

What To Do

If you cannot remember 'Baa, Baa, Black Sheep', it goes like this:

Baa, baa, black sheep,
Have you any wool?
Yes sir, yes sir, three bags full.
One for the master and one for the dame.
And one for the little boy
Who lives down the lane.

Teach them the next verse too:

Moo, moo, Jersey cow,
Have you any milk?
Yes sir, yes sir, three buckets full.
One for the master and one for the cat.
And one for the little boy who wants to get fat.

Talk about wool together, how it is shorn off the sheep and what happens next. Find a woollen garment or blanket for your children to feel.

HUMPTY DUMPTY

This nursery rhyme is a favourite of mine!

What You Need

- Eggs • Art materials

What To Do

If you cannot remember 'Humpty Dumpty', it goes like this:

Humpty Dumpty sat on a wall.
Humpty Dumpty had a great fall.
All the King's horses and all the King's men
Couldn't put Humpty together again.

There are some funny ends you can use. One of my favourites is:

Humpty Dumpty sat on a wall.
Humpty Dumpty had a great fall.
All the King's horses and all the King's men
Had bacon and eggs for breakfast again.

After your children have learnt the rhyme, why not have eggs for dinner? Keep the eggshells. Wash them and break them into small pieces with a rolling pin, then help your children make an eggshell collage of Humpty Dumpty.

Or fill half an eggshell with cotton wool. Help your children pour water onto the cotton wool to make it damp. Place the shell in an eggcup and draw on Humpty's face with felt pens. Sprinkle the top with grass seed, water regularly, and in time Humpty will grow a magnificent head of hair.

I HAD A LITTLE NUT TREE

When you teach your children nursery rhymes, you are developing their literacy skills.

What You Need

- Time

What To Do

If you cannot remember 'I Had a Little Nut Tree', it goes like this (if you can remember the tune, sing it to your children):

I had a little nut tree,
Nothing would it bear,
But a silver nutmeg and a golden pear.
The King of Spain's daughter came to visit me,
'Twas all for the sake of my little nut tree.

Macadamia nut trees are very easy to grow. They are an attractive small tree, and a useful culinary addition to your garden. If you live in a colder climate go to your local plant nursery and find out what sort of nut tree you could grow. Involve your children by making the watering of the nut tree their responsibility.

By the time the tree is big enough to bear, your children will be old enough to help crack the nuts with a hammer, nutcracker or vice.

JACK AND JILL

This is one of my son's favourite nursery rhymes.

What You Need

- Time • Bucket • Containers • Small stones

What To Do

If you cannot remember 'Jack and Jill', it goes like this:

Jack and Jill went up the hill
To fetch a pail of water.
Jack fell down and broke his crown,
And Jill came tumbling after.

Up Jack got and said to Jill,
As in his arms he caught her,
'You're not hurt, brush off the dirt,
And now we'll fetch the water.'

On a hot day, fill a large bucket with water in the garden. Your children will love pretending it is a well and filling lots of smaller buckets and containers from it. Give them some small stones, too, and they can improve their throwing skills by throwing them in the 'wishing well'. (Don't forget to supervise them carefully near the water.)

LITTLE MISS MUFFET

This is another favourite nursery rhyme.

What You Need

- Time

What To Do

If you cannot remember 'Little Miss Muffet', it goes like this:

Little Miss Muffet sat on a tuffet
Eating her curds and whey,
There came a big spider who sat down beside her
And frightened Miss Muffet away.

Today, curds and whey is called junket (see p110.)

Early one morning, go for a walk in the garden with your children. Look for spiders' webs. Drenched in dew, webs sparkle in the early morning light. Keep watching a web for a few days and see what the spider has for his dinner!

MACARONI LETTERS

Introduce your children to the letters of the alphabet with this fun activity.

What You Need

- Cardboard • Pen • PVA glue
- Uncooked macaroni

What To Do

With your children, cut out twenty-six pieces of cardboard of the same size. Write a letter of the alphabet on each piece of card. Make them nice and large.

Trace over the letters carefully with glue. Then have your children drop uncooked macaroni pieces along the glue trails.

When the cards dry, the children can play with their set of alphabet cards.

ONE, TWO, BUCKLE MY SHOE

This simple rhyme will help your children learn the basics of counting.

What You Need

- Time • Ten toy blocks

What To Do

Teach your children this rhyme:

One, two, buckle my shoe.
Three, four, close the door.
Five, six, pick up sticks.
Seven, eight, lay them straight.
Nine, ten, a big fat hen.

Place the toy blocks in a line on the floor. Count to ten, touching each block as you go. Do it a few times, then see if your children will count with you.

CAR BINGO

Prepare some simple bingo cards for the children before undertaking a long trip in the car. They will have great fun spotting various items and places, and the trip will be a pleasure for everyone.

What You Need

- Cardboard • Coloured pencils, crayons, or felt pens

What To Do

Before the trip talk to the children about some of the things they may spot on the way. These may include animals, different types of vehicles, various buildings and landscape features.

Prepare some cards with words and simple pictures on them, such as cow, dog, mountain, police car, tree, pink flowers, truck, river, bridge, stop sign.

Give each child a card and a pencil. When a child spots an item he calls it out and crosses it off his card. Only the first child to spot the item and call out its name can cross it off. The first child to cross off all the items yells 'bingo' and is the winner.

Hint!

Just draw one card and have it copied, and the copies laminated, at your local photocopying shop. Then the children simply mark their cards with a non-permanent pen and later the cards can be wiped off and used again and again.

DROP THE PENNY

A listening game to play with your children.

What You Need

- Large glass jar • Small items made from different materials, such as clothes peg, coins, comb, dice, marble, pencil, safety pin • Blindfold

What To Do

Show your children the small objects and let them listen while you drop them, one by one, into the jar.

Blindfold your children and drop the items in again, one by one, to see if they can tell you what has been dropped.

This activity is harder than it sounds—have a turn yourself and see how good your listening skills are.

FAVOURITE STORY TAPES

If your children have a favourite story that they want to read time and time again, suggest you record the story on tape so they can listen to it themselves.

What You Need

- Cassette player that young children can use
- Blank cassette tape • Story book • Bell

What To Do

Start recording the story on tape. Have the children ring the bell when it is time to turn the page. Let your children add any other sound effects.

When the taping is completed, play it back, and you will have a big laugh hearing the results.

Perhaps you could also tape some nursery rhymes or fairy tales for your children to listen to.

Nothing replaces reading books with your children and having a nice cuddle together, but good listening skills are essential for school and this activity will help develop your children's listening skills in a fun way.

GO-TOGETHERS

An activity to help develop your children's thinking and language skills.

What You Need

- Tray • Pillowcase • Objects that go together: • Cup and saucer
- Pencil and rubber • Pen and lid • Knife and fork
- Toothbrush and toothpaste • Hair brush and comb
- Needle and cotton • Key and lock
- Hammer and nail • Shoe and sock

What To Do

Explain the object of the game to your children, then put half the objects on a tray for your children to see. Place the other half of the 'go-togethers' in a pillowcase.

Your children have to reach in, feel an object, guess what it is, and then say what it goes with.

For example (sock): It feels like a sock and it goes with the shoe.

SAND NUMBERS AND LETTERS

We all know how quickly young children learn. Make some letters and numbers out of sand to help them learn easily.

What You Need

• Cardboard • PVA glue • Fine brush
• Fine beach sand • Food colouring

What To Do

This is a messy activity and is best done outdoors.

With your children, cut out thirty-six pieces of cardboard of the same size. Write a letter of the alphabet and a number from 1 to 10 on each piece of card. Make the letters and numbers large.

The children will enjoy tracing over the letters and numbers with glue on a brush. They then apply fine beach sand (this can be coloured if you wish by mixing it with food colouring and allowing it to dry).

Let the cards dry. Now the children can learn their letters and numbers by running their fingers over them and feeling the sandy shapes.

THIRTY DAYS HAS SEPTEMBER

This simple rhyme will help your children learn how many days are in each month.

What You Need

- Time

What To Do

Teach your children this rhyme:

Thirty days has September,
April, June and November.
February twenty-eight,
Thirty-one the others date.
But in leap year we assign
February twenty-nine.

WALKIE-TALKIES

Walkie-talkies make a great birthday or Christmas present for your children.

What You Need

- A set of walkie-talkies

What To Do

Consider buying a set of walkie-talkies for the children because they will give them hours of fun as they play in the garden.

The walkie-talkies will also help develop the children's language and communication skills as they play and send each other messages.

Talk to them about other ways of sending messages, such as letters in bottles, carrier pigeons, telegraphs, telephones, faxes and e-mails.

They might also like to try sending a message in a bottle or a message attached to a helium-filled balloon.

COPY THE PATTERN

Copying and recognising a pattern is an early reading skill. Children who have difficulty naming and matching colours often have difficulty learning to read.

What You Need

- Large wooden beads • Plastic threading string or long shoelaces
- White cardboard • Felt pens • Clear adhesive plastic

What To Do

Work out some simple patterns with the beads—two long yellow beads, one round red bead, two long yellow beads, and so on. Or perhaps three square blue beads, two long green beads, one small round brown bead, and then repeat. Copy the patterns onto pieces of cardboard and then cover the cardboard with plastic.

See if your children can make the same patterns by threading beads onto string. Make sure your children understand to copy the pattern from left to right—the same progression as reading. Can your children name all the bead colours and tell you what shapes the beads are? Can they continue the pattern?

Later, see if your children can create their own patterns. Perhaps they could make some for you to copy.

HICKORY DICKORY DOCK

A fun, easy-to-learn nursery rhyme.

What You Need

- Time

What To Do

If you cannot remember 'Hickory Dickory Dock', it goes like this:

Hickory dickory dock,
The mouse ran up the clock.
The clock struck one,
The mouse ran down.
Hickory dickory dock.
Tick! Tock!

Can your children tell you what comes after one o'clock? Show them the time on the kitchen clock. Talk about what happens in the morning, and what happens after lunch, and what happens after dinner. Time is a difficult concept for children to understand, so be patient!

I SPY

A good observation game that can be adapted for different age groups.

What You Need

- At least two players

What To Do

You can play this game anywhere with your children. It is a great boredom alleviator.

You say:
'I spy with my little eye something beginning with (say a letter).'

For non-spellers use a colour or a shape:
'I spy with my little eye something that's (say a colour).'
'I spy with my little eye something that's (say a shape).'

For beginner readers, it may help to use the letter pronunciation:
'I spy with my little eye something beginning with "dee".'

If your children can't guess the answer, give them clues.

I WENT SHOPPING

A fun memory game to play with your children.
A good game to play in the car on long trips, too!

What You Need

- A few players

What To Do

Sit all the players in a circle. The first person says, 'I went shopping and I bought _____.' The next player says, 'I went shopping and I bought _____ and (whatever the first player bought).'

Keep going around to see who has the best memory. Vary it by choosing specific shops e.g. 'I went to the toy shop (or fruit shop or bakery) and I bought _____.'

RHYMING IN THE CAR

Children quickly learn to recognise rhyming words, then they learn to produce words that end with the same sounds. This is an important stage in phonological awareness and essential for literacy development.

What You Need

- Car trips

What To Do

Begin by saying four or five words in a row. All of them must rhyme except for one. See who is first to call out the one that doesn't rhyme.

dog, log, frog, stone, bog   answer: stone
cat, car, mat, fat, chat   answer: car
ball, hall, small, tall, foot   answer: foot

Alternatively, say a few words and the children have to tell you if they rhyme or not.

door, floor, store   answer: yes
cat, do, elephant   answer: no
horse, course, source   answer: yes
ship, boat, canoe   answer: no

The children will enjoy making up their own lists of rhyming words to try and trick each other and Mum and Dad!

RIDDLES

Set your children some simple 'riddles' to solve. Activities like this increase their reasoning capacity and make them better at problem solving.

What You Need

- Time

What To Do

Pose riddles to your children like:

I'm thinking of something you can pedal that has three wheels. (a tricycle)

I'm thinking of something that's pretty to look at, smells sweet and grows in a garden. (a flower)

I'm thinking of something you like to lick that's cold and sweet. (an ice cream or iceblock)

I'm thinking of something you put up in the rain to stay dry. (an umbrella)

I'm thinking of something that's colourful and soft and you like to throw and catch it. (a ball)

As your children get better at solving the riddles, make the riddles harder and harder. Perhaps they would like to pose some for you.

SYLLABLE WALKS

Children need to develop phonological awareness before they can begin to learn to read. Phonological awareness is the ability to hear and manipulate sounds within words.

What You Need

- Time for walks with the children

What To Do

Go for a daily walk with the children. Recent studies have shown that children who walk or cycle to school are more alert and more focused on school work. If you can't manage morning walks in your busy day, try for a walk in the afternoon.

Play a syllable game with your children as you walk. Explain that you take one step for each syllable in a word. Start with their names. Ben-ja-min is a three-syllable name, therefore three steps. An-drew is two steps. Sam is a one-step name, but Sam-u-el is three, and so on.

When you have run out of names go onto other words. Dinosaur names are always very popular. Or think of the longest words you know. I always think of Mary Poppins and 'supercalafragalisticexpialladocious'. See if the children can work out how many steps that word would be!

The children will also enjoy clapping out the syllables, and touching different parts of their bodies as they say the syllables.

WRITING STORIES

Children need to develop knowledge of the
'language of language' before they can begin to read.

What You Need

- Paper or a scrapbook

What To Do

When you have a family excursion or special occasion encourage your children to draw pictures about it. It is a nice idea to have a special scrapbook they can keep exclusively for these special pictures.

To help them understand the 'language of language', ask them to tell you the sentence they would like you to write about their drawing. Talk to them as you write. Point to the individual words and say them out loud. Talk about any punctuation marks you use and show them what a sentence is. 'It begins with a capital letter and ends with a full stop and makes sense.'

Children need to understand the difference between a sentence and a story and this takes time. Drawing about a special occasion also helps develop children's recounting skills.

By linking these early literacy experiences to fun family events, children will enjoy drawing and learning about words and language, and these early phonological skills are the stepping stones to learning to read.

NUMBER
GAMES

SMALL TEDDY, BIG TEDDY

Introduce your children to the concepts of big and small from an early age.

What You Need

- A large teddy bear
- A small teddy bear

What To Do

Play with the teddy bears with your child. Call the large teddy bear 'big teddy' and the small teddy bear 'small teddy'. (Of course, you don't have to use teddy bears, any pair of soft toys will do—just make sure they are different sizes.)

Tell your child the teddy bears are going to hide. 'Hide' both bears in sight of your child. Their hiding places should be obvious e.g. hide one teddy on a cushion, hide another by the leg of a chair. Ask your child to find big teddy. When your child has done that, ask her to find small teddy. Give her lots of praise when she gets it right. Do this several times.

You'll be surprised how quickly your child will learn to distinguish between the two bears. Start using the words 'big' and 'small' when talking to your child about other objects.

CLOTHES PEG SORTING

A simple colour sorting game to play with your children.
Sorting colours is the first step in learning to name them.

What You Need

- Plastic clothes pegs of different colours • Ice-cream containers

What To Do

Clip a different-coloured peg onto the side of each container. Ask your children to sort the pegs by colour into the correct container. When they have finished this, show them how to clip the pegs around the side of the container. (This will be difficult for some children, but persist over time as they need strong finger muscles to begin writing.)

Later, you can help them count the pegs to find which container holds the most pegs. Can they name their colours yet? If not, play colour-learning games with them.

GARAGES

Learning how to sort objects into sizes is an important mathematical skill. This activity will help teach your young children how to do this in a fun way.

What You Need

- Toy cars of various sizes
- Boxes of various sizes

What To Do

Match the boxes to the sizes of the cars or else cut doorways in the boxes to fit the different-sized cars.

Your children will have lots of fun driving the cars into the right garages. See if they can order the cars from the smallest to the largest. Practise counting how many cars there are altogether, too!

LARGE AND SMALL

An activity to help younger children begin to sort and classify.

What You Need

- Tray • Large and small boxes e.g. apple box, shoebox
  - Big and small versions of the same objects

large toy car	small matchbox car
large comb	small comb
large brush	small brush
tablespoon	teaspoon
large stone	small stone
large leaf	small leaf

What To Do

Place the items on a tray. Ask one child to find an object, then find its smaller or larger version. Tell them to put the small items in the shoebox and the large items in the apple box.

MATCHING GAMES

Make sure your children have lots of opportunities to try matching objects—this is an important mathematical skill.

What You Need

- Large box
- Find lots of objects to match:
  Pair of socks
  Clothes pegs
  Buttons
  Toys
  Shoes
  Cutlery
  Gloves

What To Do

Put all the pairs in a large box. Ask your children to match all the pairs.

When that's done, have your children help you sort the washing, and find everyone's pairs of socks.

OUTLINES

An activity to help younger children learn to compare size.

What You Need

• Paper • Pencil • Scissors

What To Do

Have each child place a hand on a piece of paper and spread their fingers. Trace around the outline of the hand. Cut the outline out.

Now do the same to your own hand and the hands of other members of the family. Let your children compare the hand outlines, then line them up from smallest to largest.

Do the same with the family's feet (after they have bathed or showered!).

Keep your children's hand and foot outlines so you can compare them with new ones in a year or so. You'll be amazed at how much they've grown.

2+

POURING AND MEASURING

A fun measuring activity for children.

What You Need

- A sheet or tablecloth • A large plastic tub
- Mixture of rice, dried beans, rolled oats, pasta, sago

What To Do

Fill the tub with the dry food and put the tub on the sheet on the floor. Add toys from your children's sandpit to the tub, as well as funnels, cups, spoons of different sizes, strainers and jugs.

Encourage your children to fill the utensils with the dry food. They may also enjoy using trucks, cars, diggers and animals in the tub. The different mixtures make great loads for small trucks and backhoes.

Help your children to create mountains, valleys and other interesting landscapes for toy animals, or even a moonscape or dinosaur world.

Make sure the tub is securely covered after playing or, better still, transfer the contents to sealed containers to stop vermin sharing the fun.

ZANY MATCH-UPS

This is a fun matching game for younger children.

What You Need

- Small items such as blocks, bobby pins, buttons, comb, cotton reel, knife, matchbox, pegs, pen, spoon, pencil, pins, rubber bands, safety pin, scissors, screwdriver
- Large sheet of cardboard • Contact
- Small box or container
- Coloured felt pens or pencils

What To Do

Place each object on the cardboard and trace around it. If an object is coloured, use the same colour for the outline. Cover the cardboard with contact to keep it clean. Put the objects in a container.

Ask your children to match the objects to the outlines. Ask them questions such as:

How many red things are there?
How many things are made of metal?
Can you find me something that's made of plastic?

Later, your children might like to see how fast they can match the objects to their outlines, or see if they can beat an egg timer.

3+

COUNT THE APPLE SEEDS

An easy, fun way to teach your children numbers.

What You Need

- Apple • Knife

What To Do

With your children watching, cut the apple in half. Talk about the tiny seeds that are found inside apples. Explain that new plants grow from seeds.

Have the children remove the apple seeds (they may need your help). Can they count the seeds?

When the children have finished examining the seeds, they can eat the apple!

FISHING FUN

A fun way to practise counting and to make size comparisons.

What You Need

- Coloured cardboard • Scissors • Paper clips • Magnet
- Ruler or a short length of dowel • String

What To Do

Cut out lots of cardboard fish. Be imaginative and make them different shapes, sizes and colours. Slide a paper clip on each fish's 'mouth'. Tie a magnet onto the ruler or length of dowel with some string. Your children will love catching the fish and telling you about them. Ask them to show you all the red fish, or all the blue or green fish. Next, see if they can show you the largest or smallest fish. Talk about all the colours and do lots of counting.

Follow up the fishing game with fish and chips for tea!

MY DAY

Young children find learning to tell the time
very difficult. Before they can understand,
they must acquire a sense of event sequence.
Activities like this one will help.

What You Need

- A long strip of paper
- Felt pens or coloured pencils

What To Do

Discuss with your children the sorts of things they do in a normal day. Then give them a strip of paper each and some coloured pens or pencils.

Ask them to draw a sun at one end of the paper and the moon and stars at the other, for the beginning and end of the day. Next, they draw in their day—when they get up, have breakfast, get dressed, go to pre-school, things they do there, come home, play outside, have their bath, have dinner, play or watch TV, brush their teeth, have stories, go to bed. Hang their 'my day' picture in their bedroom and talk about it together.

Hang a calendar in their room. If they are looking forward to a particular event, perhaps a birthday party or having a friend sleep over, you can cross off the days as they pass.

NUMBER STOPS

This activity uses up lots of energy and is educational at the same time! It's best played with several children.

What You Need

- Cardboard • Scissors
- Thick marker

What To Do

Cut out ten large cardboard 'number stops'. Write the numbers 1 to 10 on them. If you want to re-use the number stops, it's a good idea to have them laminated before you start the game.

Place the number stops around your backyard and gather the children around you. Explain that you're going to make ten statements, such as 'This morning, I bought six eggs' and 'I saw three birds in the park'.

Whenever the children hear a number, they must run to the corresponding number stop. The first to stand on the correct number spot wins one point. The winner is the child with the most points at the end of the game.

SORTING TIME

Sorting things into groups or sets is a basic mathematical skill. As your toddlers help you sort the washing they are gaining important sorting skills.

What You Need

- Washing to sort

What To Do

Sort out the family's washing on your bed so there's plenty of room to spread it all out. Work out with your children where each person's pile will be. Encourage your young children to verbalise, 'That's where we put Daddy's things' and 'My things go here'.

Then your children can help you put the items in the correct piles and find pairs of socks. When all the sorting is completed they can help carry each person's pile to their bedroom.

BIG FEET

*Another fun activity that helps your children
compare sizes and learn mathematical terms.*

What You Need

- Plastic ice-cream container
  lids or strong cardboard
  - Elastic • Felt pen

What To Do

Draw around your feet (or your partner's). Cut out the feet and attach elastic so your children can wear the feet and discover what it's like to have 'big feet'.

When you are walking on the beach or in the sandpit compare all the family's footprints. Can they tell you who has the largest feet, the smallest etc.?

4+

BUTTONS

A sorting game which helps your children work out similarities and differences.

What You Need

- Lots of assorted buttons in a container
  - Egg cartons or ice-cube trays

What To Do

If you don't have lots of buttons of different sizes, shapes and colours in your button box, charity shops sell them cheaply.

Give the buttons to your children to sort according to their own criteria. Ask them to explain to you what they have done.

If they are having difficulty with this, offer some suggestions such as:

Could you sort them into different colours?
Could you find the ones with two holes, and then the ones with four holes?
Could you put all the metal ones together?

With younger children, colour the bottom of an egg carton with different colours and your children can sort the buttons into the correct holes.

MY WEEK

*This activity will help your child learn the days of the week
and understand more about the passing of time.*

What You Need

- A long piece of paper
- Felt pens or coloured pencils

What To Do

Divide the piece of paper into seven sections with your pen. Write the days of the week on the paper, starting with Sunday.

Talk to your child about things he does regularly on certain days. 'On Monday you come to tennis with Mum.' 'On Wednesday you go to kindergarten.' 'On Saturday Dad takes you to gym class.'

Have your child draw in each section the things he enjoys doing most on that day.

At the end of the week hang it in his bedroom and talk about it together using language like 'yesterday', 'tomorrow', 'last week', 'next week', 'night', 'day' and so on.

NUMBER MATCH

A simple activity to help young children learn numbers.

What You Need

- Paper • Coloured felt pen

What To Do

Write the numbers 1 to 5 all over a piece of paper. Ask your children to draw lines to match up pairs of numbers. Make it even harder by drawing the numbers in different colours e.g. a blue 5 and a yellow 5, a green 3 and a pink 3.

Can your children tell you what the numbers are? Can they find three yellow objects in their toy box? Five blue pegs in the peg basket? Two green leaves in the garden?

When your children know the numbers 1 to 5, add 6 to 10 also.

PAPER-CLIP COUNTING

A fun hands-on counting game.

What You Need

- Ten pieces of cardboard about 12 cm (5 in) square
- Felt pens • Paper clips or clothes pegs

What To Do

Number each of the pieces of cardboard from 1 to 10. Put the corresponding number of dots on each piece of cardboard so your children can count the dots if they cannot yet recognise numbers.

See if you children can slide the correct number of paper clips onto each piece of cardboard. When they are finished check to see if they are right. Older children can play this game with numbers to 20 or higher.

4+

SHAPE MOBILES

Help you children learn geometric shapes with this balancing activity.

What You Need

- Stiff cardboard or polystyrene trays • Scissors
- Paints and coloured pencils • Sticky tape
- String • Wire coat-hangers

What To Do

Help your children draw and cut out simple geometric shapes—circles, squares, rectangles and triangles—from the cardboard. Cut two of each shape. Let your children decorate the shapes.

Next, cut a slit in the centre of each one and joint them at right angles (use the sticky tape to hold them in place).

Your children will enjoy hanging up the shapes on a wire coat-hanger to make a shape mobile. Watch the shapes move and spin in the breeze!

WEIGHING

This activity will help your children understand terms such as 'lightest' and 'heaviest'.

What You Need

- Bathroom scales • Kitchen scales
  - Various items to weigh
  - Paper • Coloured pencils

What To Do

Begin by weighing all the members of your family. Your children can draw a picture of each person and you can help them write the person's weight on their picture. Discuss who is the heaviest and who is the lightest.

Next, raid the pantry and find tins and packs of various shapes and weights. Let your children weigh them and together work out which are the heaviest and which are the lightest items. Try to find items that weigh the same but are different shapes or sizes, perhaps a tin of baked beans and a packet of flour.

GAMES TO PLAY

FALLING-DOWN GAME

A fun game for very young children to play.

What You Need

- Children • Music
- Room to play safely

What To Do

Play some music and have the children dance. When you stop the music everyone falls down.

When you start the music, everyone jumps up and starts dancing again.

ONE ELEPHANT WENT BALANCING

A party game that littlies will love to play.

What You Need

- A group of small children
- A long piece of string or rope

What To Do

Lay a long piece of string on the floor. The children stand around the string, but not on it.

If you know the tune, sing it for the children, otherwise teach it as a chant. Choose one child to be the first 'elephant' and the children do the choosing after that. The 'elephant' steps on the piece of string. When everyone sings the last line of the first verse, the 'elephant' points to one child to come and join him on the string.

One elephant went balancing
From foot to foot on a piece of string.
It had such enormous fun
That it called for another elephant to come.

The game continues until you decide there's enough children on the string. The last verse is:

Five elephants went balancing
From foot to foot on a piece of string.
All of a sudden the piece of string broke,
And down came all of the elephant folk!

Young children will, of course, love the last part when they all fall down on top of one another!

RING A ROSY

Young children love this fun falling-down game.

What You Need

- Children • Room to play safely

What To Do

This is a good game to play outside on the grass.

Everyone hold hands and dances around singing:

Ring a ring a rosy,
A pocket full of posy,
Ah tishoo, ah tishoo,
We all fall down.

Everyone falls down.

Then, sitting on the ground everyone sings:

Picking all the daisies, the daisies, the daisies,
Picking all the daisies,
We all jump up!

Repeat a few times until everyone is exhausted!

BIRTHDAY PIÑATA

Make a Mexican piñata with your children to use at their next birthday party.

What You Need

- A balloon • Wallpaper paste
- Newspaper and coloured paper
- Streamers • Paint • Lollies

What To Do

Blow up the balloon if your children can't manage this, and then begin the papier mâché process. Your children can help cut or tear the newspaper into strips. Next, dip the strips in the glue and paste them over the balloon. Papier mâché is best done over a few days to allow the layers to dry. Hang the balloon from the clothes line to dry really well.

When the papier mâché is thick enough, burst the balloon and carefully cut a hole in the top of the papier mâché. Decorate the papier mâché with colourful paints and bright patterns and hang streamers from the bottom. Fill with sweets.

At the party, hang up the piñata and let the children take it in turns to hit it with a stick (blindfolds add an extra challenge) until it breaks and the sweets fall out. Lots of fun!

SHOPPING

Although it is tempting to leave young children at home when you shop for the groceries, it can be made into a learning experience for them.

What You Need

- Supermarket catalogues
  - Paper • Pencil

What To Do

Before you do your grocery shopping, sit down with the children and do some brainstorming about what you need. I find my son is much better than me at remembering what we have run out of—especially if it is something he likes! Write the items down for younger children—older children can write the shopping list for you.

If you have any advertising from your local supermarket look at the specials with the children and decide if you are going to buy any. Talk about budgets and the amount you have to spend. Children need to understand that we plan what we buy and why.

Planning shopping trips also provides opportunities to talk about balanced diets and why you buy certain items.

Perhaps older children could assist in planning some meals they would like to help prepare, and you can add what you would need to the shopping list. Littlies will enjoy finding items as you shop and putting them into the trolley for you. The children can also help sort out the groceries when you come home.

THE SILENT GAME

*A wonderful game for harassed and tired
parents travelling with children in their car!*

What You Need

- Children in the car

What To Do

This is a very quiet game! Perfect for those times in the car when you are ready to stop the car and either leave it yourself or leave the passengers!

Tell the children that the first person to break the silence loses that round. Time it by kilometres, the next petrol station you pass, the next dog you see, or so on. Play it every now and then on a long trip and someone can be the scorer. At the end of the trip see who was the best at being quiet, and who broke the silence the most. (It probably won't be a surprise!)

BIRD'S NEST GAME

A fast and lively game to play with three or more children.

What You Need

- Three plastic hoops • Five beanbags (fill old socks with sand, rice or dried beans to make quick and easy beanbags)

What To Do

Explain to the children that the hoops are pretend birds' nests and that the beanbags are the eggs. Put the beanbags in the centre of the room and put the three hoops around them—make sure the hoops are all the same distance from the beanbags.

Choose three children to have the first turn—they each stand in their 'nest' or hoop. When you say 'go' the children each run in, pick up a beanbag and run back and place it in their nest. They then run back for another one. When the beanbags have gone from the middle they can 'steal' them from each other's nests. When a child has three eggs in their nest they sit down on them and yell 'bird's nest' and win the game. Remind the players that only one beanbag at a time can be placed in the nest and that they must be put in, not thrown from a distance.

This game is fast and furious and is just as funny for the onlookers as for the players. It moves so fast I often think it should be called 'perpetual motion'!

HEY, MR CROCODILE!

A good game to play at children's parties or any time a group of kids is together.

What You Need

- Children

What To Do

Choose one child to be Mr Crocodile. The rest of the children line up on the other side of an imaginary river. They then begin asking Mr Crocodile if they can cross the river:

Hey, Mr Crocodile, can we cross the water
To see your lovely daughter
Floating in the water
Like a cup and saucer?

Mr Crocodile replies:

Yes, if you're wearing red! (Or shoes, buttons, hair ribbons etc.)

Any child wearing red (or shoes, buttons, hair ribbons etc.) crosses the river.

I WROTE A LETTER

I'm sure nearly everyone has played this game at birthday parties.
Provide a handkerchief for the 'letter', or an envelope if you wish.

What You Need

- Children • Handkerchief or envelope

What To Do

The children sit down in a circle and join hands. Choose a child to have the first turn. The child walks around the circle with the hanky while everyone chants or sings:

I wrote a letter to my love
And on the way I dropped it.
Someone must have picked it up
And put it in their pocket.
It's you! It's you! It's you!

When the last line is sung, the walking child drops the hanky behind another child's back. When that child realises it's behind her back, she jumps up and chases the first child around the circle. The first child must run to the empty place and sit down before he is tagged.

The child who was chasing then has the next turn.

OLD MOTHER WITCH

An old group game which makes a great Halloween night game.

What You Need

- Children

What To Do

The children sit down in a circle and join hands. Choose a child to have the first turn. The child walks around the inside of the circle while the other children chant:

Old Mother Witch couldn't find her stitch,
Rode her broomstick round and round,
Then asked another friend to town,
Whoosh, whoosh, whoosh, whoosh, wham!

On 'wham' the child points his arm like a witch's wand at another child and that child then becomes Old Mother Witch!

SARDINES

*A very funny game that is great to play at family
gatherings or with a large group of children.*

What You Need

- A house with lots of hiding places

What To Do

One person is chosen to be the 'sardine', and goes to hide while the rest of the players close their eyes and count to 100. They then go and look for the sardine.

When the sardine is found by someone, that person must squeeze into the sardine's hiding place with the sardine. (Don't forget to remind the players before they start to keep as quiet as possible while they are hiding—giggling is a real give-away!) As each player finds the sardine, they must squeeze into the same hiding place. Finally everyone is there—squeezed in like a tin of sardines!

The person who found the sardine first, becomes the next sardine.

3

TREASURE HUNT

A fun party game for the small fry.

What You Need

- Lots of players • Some treasure—perhaps a coin

What To Do

Choose one child to be the first 'treasure hunter'.

All the others sit in a circle on the floor around the treasure hunter. The players pass the 'treasure' around the circle from hand to hand and the treasure hunter has to point to who has the treasure. Encourage the children to make it harder by pretending to pass the treasure even when they're not.

The treasure hunter only has three guesses as this keeps the game moving and means everyone has a turn. (Young children find it difficult to wait for their turn.) The person with the treasure becomes the next treasure hunter.

WHO STOLE THE COOKIE?

This party game develops memory and verbal skills.

What You Need

- A group of children

What To Do

Sit the children in a circle. Start the rhythm of the game by doing one clap of hands and then a knee tap i.e. clap tap, clap tap. Have the children imitate you. When the children are all following the rhythm, teach them the chant:

Who stole the cookie from the cookie jar?

Name a child:
Tom stole the cookie from the cookie jar.

Tom says:
Who me?

The group responds with:
Yes, you!

Tom says:
Couldn't be!

The group says:
Then who?

Tom chooses the next player and the game continues.

LITTLE TOMMY TITTLEMOUSE

A game to play at a children's party or just with a group of children.

What You Need

- Children

What To Do

The children sit down in a circle and join hands. Choose a child to have the first turn at being 'Tommy Tittlemouse'. This child sits in the middle of the circle and closes her eyes. Choose another child to be the first to have his voice identified. The children in the circle then chant:

Little Tommy Tittlemouse
Sat inside his little house.
Someone's knocking, me oh my,
Someone's calling, 'It is I!'

The child picked to have his voice identified says the 'It is I' line. The child in the circle has to try to identify the speaker. The speaker then has a turn at being Tommy Tittlemouse.

ORANGES AND LEMONS

An oldie but a goldie! A game most of us played at birthday parties when we were young. Teach it to your children and it will be just as popular today as it was years ago.

What You Need

- Children

What To Do

Choose two tall children to form an archway with their hands. They then decide with an adult which one is going to be the 'orange' and which the 'lemon'. The other children make a line behind a leader. They then walk through the archway chanting:

> Oranges and lemons say the bells of St Clements.
> You owe me five farthings say the bells of St Martins.
> When will you pay me say the bells of Old Bailey?
> When I grow rich say the bells of Shoreditch.
> Here comes a candle to light you to bed.
> Here comes a chopper to chop off your—your—your—your—your—head!

On the final 'head' the archway is lowered and a child is caught. The archway children then take the 'caught' child away and ask her if she wants to be an orange or a lemon (keep it a secret which archway child is which). When the child has chosen, she lines up behind that archway child. When all the children have been caught in the archway and have chosen to be an orange or a lemon, they form two teams and have a tug-of-war!

POSSUMS IN THE TREE

A fast-moving game to play in the backyard with a group of children.

What You Need

- Lots of children • Space to run

What To Do

Divide the children into groups of three. Two children in each group become the tree by placing their hands on each other's shoulders, thus forming a tree with a hollow in the middle. The third child in each trio becomes the possum in the tree (standing between the tree).

Keep a few children out as extra possums who don't have trees. When you clap or whistle, all the possums have to run to a new tree, giving the extra possums a chance to capture a tree.

Make sure all the children have a turn at being the possums as well as the trees.

SCIENCE CENTRES

Our capital cities now have wonderful hands-on science centres which are great for a family day out. If you haven't visited one, plan to soon and you will enjoy the interesting and challenging activities.

What You Need

- Time • Access to a science centre

What To Do

We recently visited the Brisbane Science Centre and had a wonderful day. The admission is very, very reasonable—in fact a whole family pass for twelve months is cheaper than one adult entry into most of the large theme parks—and the kids tried everything!

Wear your most comfortable shoes, take a backpack with food and cold drinks, and be prepared to use those old 'grey cells'. (It's most embarrassing to have things explained to you by a six-year-old!)

We were able to obtain pass-outs to have a picnic lunch and, apart from that, we were there for the whole day and still didn't have a chance to do everything.

If only school was like that, I'm sure I would have enjoyed science so much more.

TENPIN BOWLING

*An evening at your local tenpin bowling alley
is an activity that children and adults can enjoy.*

What You Need

- Time • Money

What To Do

Tenpin bowling is a great game for the whole family to enjoy together and is quite inexpensive. Our local bowling alley often has discount vouchers printed on the back of our local supermarket's dockets.

You can hire the special shoes at the bowling alley and the balls are provided. We like to go with at least one other family so we can have a kids lane with buffers and a lane for the adults.

Smaller children can simply roll their bowling balls down a stand, so they don't have to pick up the heavy balls. Let the children use a lane with the gutters covered, they'll enjoy the game much more.

THE FARMER IN THE DELL

4

A traditional game that children always love to play at a party or group gathering.

What You Need

- Lots of children

What To Do

Begin by standing the children in a circle. Choose a 'farmer' to stand in the middle. The song begins. As each new character is introduced, choose a child to play that role in the middle of the circle.

The farmer in the dell, the farmer in the dell,
Hi, ho, the dairy-o, the farmer in the dell.
The farmer takes a wife, the farmer takes a wife,
Hi, ho, the dairy-o, the farmer takes a wife.

The song continues:

The wife takes a child etc.
The child takes a nurse etc.
The nurse takes a dog etc.
The dog takes a cat etc.
The cat takes a mouse etc.
The mouse takes some cheese etc.
We all eat the cheese etc.

Everyone rushes in to 'eat' the cheese. (Don't choose a timid child to be the cheese, or they may not enjoy being eaten!)

4+

THREE-LEGGED RACES

An old Sunday School picnic favourite from my childhood.

What You Need

- Old pantihose or scarves
- At least four children

What To Do

Mark out a starting and a finishing line.

The children divide into pairs. Make sure they remove their shoes, and then tie each pair of children firmly together around their ankles with a scarf or pair of old pantihose. The children hold each other around the waist.

Line up all the contestants and begin the race. If the children are having difficulties, remind them to start walking by moving their joined legs together first. Speed is not essential at first—it's more important to get a rhythm going.

Give everyone lots of practice until they get the hang of it!

WHO'S MISSING?

A game to develop thinking skills.

What You Need

- A group of children

What To Do

The children sit in a circle and one child is sent away where he cannot see or hear what is happening.

Another child is chosen from the group to go and hide out of sight. Make sure that all the remaining children are certain who is hiding. Then, the first child is allowed to return, and looks around the circle to try to remember who is missing. If he cannot remember, the other children can offer clues e.g. they can describe something the hidden child is wearing, or say the first letter of her name. Allow three clues only. If the first child has not guessed, the hidden child comes out of hiding and the game starts all over again with two more children.

OUTDOOR
ACTIVITIES

ICEBERG PLAY

Great fun on a hot day.

What You Need

- Large container for water play
- Balloons of various shapes
- Food colouring • Eye-droppers

What To Do

Buy a packet of assorted balloons and select some different shapes. Fill each with water and place them in the freezer for a couple of days.

When they are frozen solid, cut away the balloon, leaving the frozen shape.

Place the iced shapes into your children's wading pool, large dish or even a baby bath. Your children will have lots of fun dropping food colouring onto the frozen shapes with the eye-dropper and watching the colours change.

Another time you can fill plastic containers with coloured water for a different experience.

Your children will be fascinated by these colourful 'icebergs'.

SANDPIT ZOO

Young children are fascinated with zoos. Help your children make a toy animal zoo in the sandpit.

What You Need

- Boxes • Polystyrene cups • Scissors • Sticky tape
- Drinking straws • Poster or acrylic paints • Card
- Lids • Small pieces of plants • Toy zoo animals

What To Do

If your children haven't visited a zoo take them along. Most cities have zoos you can visit.

After the visit help them make a zoo in the sandpit. Help them cut holes in the boxes and cups to make animal homes and let them paint them. Next, sticky tape the straws together to make fences for the zoo.

Use a piece of card to smooth down paths for the visitors to walk on and add the plants and flowers to make gardens. Help the children fill the lids with water and bury them in the sand to make ponds and drinking pools for the animals.

Arrange the animals in the zoo and leave the children to have a great time playing with their sandpit zoo.

SANDPITS

Probably the best thing we ever did for our son was to build him a large sandpit in our garden. With my background as a pre-school teacher I made sure my husband and father (the sandpit builders) did it properly.

What You Need

- Half logs of treated pine
- Gravel • White beach sand

What To Do

Make a very large, very deep hole and box it in well. Attach half logs of treated pine around the top. Place gravel in the bottom for good drainage and add white beach sand on top.

Make sure your sandpit is large enough to accommodate digging toys, and several small people.

Andrew is now six and a half and has enjoyed his sandpit for nearly five years. He still plays in it and, whenever we make noises about filling it in, he manages to convince us that he will still need it for some time.

If you have a small child please build them a sandpit. Children need the opportunity to dig, mix, play with sand and water, and be allowed to make a mess. They can always have a bath when they have finished playing!

SPONGE TARGETS

Lots of fun for the whole family on hot days.

What You Need

- Sponge offcuts
- Chalk • Bucket

What To Do

Draw a clown's face or some other target on the brick walls of the house. Fill a bucket with water, dip the sponge pieces in the water and take it in turns to throw them at the target and 'wipe' it out. Great for a hot day as everyone gets nice and wet while you do it.

WATER PLAY

Young children never tire of playing with water. Give your children lots of props for their wading pool and they will be happily occupied for hours on a hot day. Remember, however, that young children must always be supervised near water.

What You Need

- Wading pool • Hose • A selection of plastic containers, measuring cups, plastic toys, large and small buckets, funnels, colanders, egg beater, plastic tubing, corks, tins with holes punched in them, sponges, PVC conduit and anything else you can think of!

What To Do

Place your children's wading pool (or baby bath or a large dish) in a shady part of the garden on a hot day. Turn on the hose and let them fill the pool (it's best if they are wearing their swimming costumes!).

Provide lots of toys for the wading pool and your children will have a great time.

For a change, add some food colouring to the water—this way they can see the water clearly as they pour and measure.

BACKYARD MAZES

*Most young children love to wiggle and squirm
through small places. Try this activity in the backyard.*

What You Need

- Garden furniture • Cardboard boxes
- Buckets • String or thin rope

What To Do

Set up a backyard maze by using some of your outdoor furniture. The children have to crawl underneath the furniture and reach the end of the maze in a set amount of time.

Increase the difficulty by placing some obstacles in their way, such as rope tied across two chairs that they have to wriggle under or climb over and not touch. Or you might place a bucket of water on one of the chairs. The children have to wriggle under the bucket without touching it, or it might move and spill.

Give older children a handicap by making them complete the maze in a much shorter time or make them carry a plastic cup of water. If they spill some of the water they have to fill up the cup and start again.

See if the children can come up with some new ideas to add to the maze!

BATS AND BALLS

Developing hand-eye coordination skills early will help your children's ability to play sports such as tennis, cricket, golf, softball and baseball when they are older.

What You Need

- Old pantihose • Wire coat-hangers
- Masking or insulating tape • Tennis ball

What To Do

Bend the coat-hanger into the shape of a racquet and straighten the bent handle. Re-bend the handle over so it is narrower and longer than before.

Cut one leg off the pantihose and keep for later. Pull the other leg over the racquet until taut, then wrap the rest of the pantihose around the handle. Cover with the tape until the handle is firm and easy to hold.

Put a tennis ball in the toe of the spare pantihose leg and tie from a tree branch, the clothes line, or a hook.

Your children will have lots of fun hitting the ball backwards and forwards with the soft bat. Make two bats so your children can hit with you or a friend or sibling. The bats are so soft no one will get hurt if they're accidentally hit.

CARDBOARD TUNNELS

Cardboard boxes are great because they are free and are also terrific for children's creative play. Fill up your car with boxes from your local fruit shop or electrical store and let the children make a great tunnel maze in your backyard.

What You Need

- Cardboard sheets or boxes of different shapes and sizes
- Strong masking or insulating tape

What To Do

Help the children open out different sides of boxes and join them together to make tunnels. Long boxes can have a hole cut in the side so another box can be fitted into it. Use the masking or insulating tape to hold the boxes firmly together. Use a variety of boxes of different shapes and sizes to make the tunnel maze a real challenge.

When the tunnels are finished the children might enjoy decorating them with some acrylic paints. They could even make textured tunnels with different surfaces to crawl along—bubble wrap, towels, carpet, hessian mats or just the grass.

If they want a spooky tunnel they could hang things from the roof, such as wet plastic gloves, lengths of cellophane, crepe paper, or partly blown-up balloons.

Let them keep their tunnels for a few days. By then their interest will probably have waned and you can taken the whole lot to the tip and let the grass grow again!

DAY AT THE BEACH

A day at the beach is a great way to spend some quality time together as a family.

What You Need

- Swimming costumes • Sunscreen
- Beach umbrella • Hats
- Lots of cool drinks, fruit and other snacks
- Buckets, spades, ball • Towels

What To Do

Many parents have concerns about sun safety but today there is excellent sun-protective clothing available for adults and children. Don't forget lots of sunscreen and hats as well. My son has worn legionnaire's caps made of sun-protective fabric that tie on since he was a baby, and he still wears them at the beach with no fuss.

We never go to the beach without buckets and spades as we like to gather interesting things to bring home, such as seaweed, small pieces of driftwood, shells, stones and other bits and pieces.

Another wonderful aspect of beach visits for children is the ease with which they make new friends. It doesn't take long for children to gather together to ride their boogie boards, make dams or build sandcastles.

Take a good book and a low beach chair so you can read comfortably, but still supervise the children. Make sure they understand beach and water safety from an early age. Relax and enjoy!

2

DUCK, DUCK, GOOSE

A fun game to play with a group of children.

What You Need

- Children • Space to run

What To Do

The children sit down in a circle and join hands. One child is chosen to be 'it'. He walks around behind the children, tapping each child on the head as he passes and saying 'duck', 'duck', 'duck'. When he taps someone on the head and says 'goose', the goose jumps up and chases the first child around the circle. If the first child is tagged before he sits down in the goose's empty spot he goes into the middle of the circle and becomes a 'plum pudding'.

The goose then is 'it' and the game continues until all the children have had a turn.

At the end everyone can pretend to eat any plum pudding in the middle of the circle.

FAMILY PICNICS

*Everyone loves a picnic! A picnic's a terrific way
to spend some happy, relaxed time with the kids.*

What You Need

- Picnic basket • Lots of food and drinks
- Rug, pillows • Balls, cricket bat, etc.
- Damp face washers or pre-moistened
  towelettes for sticky fingers

What To Do

I have a large picnic basket that I keep packed with plastic plates, cups, thermos, sugar, salt and pepper, tablecloth, serviettes, and tea towels, so packing a quick picnic lunch is easy.

Take food which travels well and pack it in an esky with lots of freezer blocks—no one wants an upset tummy after a picnic. Take more food and drink than you think you will need, as everyone always gets hungry in the open air.

We love marinated chicken wings or drumsticks, lots of fruit and something yummy for dessert. Call in to your local hot-bread shop on the way and stock up with delicious breads or rolls.

Take a container with salad vegies, such as celery and carrot sticks, radishes and baby tomatoes, and bring along some mayonnaise with a little curry powder added for dipping, or a commercially made dip.

FOLLOW THE LEADER

Play a game of follow the leader with your littlies!

What You Need

• Time • Room to play

What To Do

Line the littlies up and show them how to play follow the leader. Try to move in lots of different ways such as skipping (they will have trouble with this one, but it's hilarious watching them try), jumping, walking sideways, walking backwards, taking little fairy steps or giant steps, running, crawling and so on.

When you run out of ideas one of the children can be the leader.

JUMPSCOTCH

*Younger children find traditional hopscotch too difficult. Develop their
balance and coordination with the simpler jumpscotch.*

What You Need

- Chalk • Stone or beanbag

What To Do

Draw a hopscotch pattern on the concrete with chalk, making sure the spaces are large enough for
your children to jump in.

Show your children how to jump with their feet together from space to space until they reach the
end of the jumpscotch. Show them how to turn around at the end and then jump back. When
they have mastered this, play the game together using a stone or beanbag to throw. Your children
must not jump in the space where the stone lies, but must pass it. They pick up the stone on their
way back.

LET'S GO OUT

So often outings with children involve spending lots of money
but there are many places you can take young children for free.
For them what's important is that you are spending time with them.

What You Need

- A picnic lunch • A rug

What To Do

The excursion venue will depend on your child's age and experience. For many young children the local park is a great outing. Pack a ball and a book for when they tire of playing on the playground equipment and don't forget sunscreen and a hat.

Older children might enjoy an outing to a beach, river, dam or a local swimming hole. Pack swimming costumes in summer and a ball to kick and throw in winter. If you all enjoy fishing take some fishing gear.

The main thing is that a picnic is a great way for the family to enjoy each other's company without spending a great deal of money.

SEE-SAW MARJORY DAW

Make a simple but very effective see-saw at home with junk materials and the children will love it. Make sure that you discuss the safety aspects with your children and supervise carefully.

What You Need

- Small wooden cable reel—often available from phone or electricity companies • Styrofoam blocks • Old car tyres
- A plank of wood—sanded well and treated with a mixture of linseed oil and turps to preserve it for outside use

What To Do

Place the cable reel on its side in an open, grassy position in the garden. Wedge a block of styrofoam or a tyre on either side of it to prevent the cable reel moving. Put the plank across the cable reel and position a tyre under both ends to cushion the impact and to prevent the children's feet being caught under the ends of the plank.

The children will love having their own see-saw in the garden. Teach them the old nursery rhyme:

See-saw, Marjory Daw,
Johnny shall have a new master.
He shall have but a penny a day,
Because he can't work any faster.

229

SENSORY WALKS

Make up a sensory walk for your young children to experience.

What You Need

Shallow plastic containers containing:
- Playdough • Gloop • Cooked rice • Uncooked rice
- Seeds or grain • Mud • Wet sand • Water
- Finger paint • Sandpaper • Carpet • Bubble wrap

What To Do

Assemble all or some of the items above, or think of your own interesting mix of textures. Put the plastic containers out on the lawn with a different substance in each. Have the children remove their shoes and socks, and move along the texture walk.

Encourage their vocabulary by asking them what each substance or texture feels like.

Make the last container the finger paint and spread some paper beside it. That way you can print their little footprints for special wrapping paper or to keep for posterity!

SOAPY WATER

Use up your old soap pieces while your children have a ball making bubbles.

What You Need

- A large washing-up dish • Old pieces of soap
- Graters, whisks, egg beaters, jugs, plastic cups, bowls

What To Do

One a nice sunny day, fill a dish with water and place old pieces of soap in it. Put it out on the lawn and the children will have a great time making wonderful soapy bubbles with whisks and egg beaters.

If they have some plastic dolls they can wash them in the soapy water too, or they can simply enjoy measuring and pouring with some plastic containers.

Important!

Any activity involving water and young children must be carefully supervised at all times.

2+

SQUIRT TARGETS

A terrific hot weather activity for the little squirts in your family!

What You Need

- Plastic squirt bottles, such as old shampoo bottles
  or old cleaning bottles (make sure they are
  really well washed out) • Coloured chalk

What To Do

Use all your creativity to draw a colourful clown, face, or other image on concrete or pavers for the children to 'squirt' out.

Put the children in their swimming costumes and give them a variety of plastic squirt bottles filled with water.

They will love squirting the water to rub out the face!

This is a wonderful way to spend a hot day, but it's also an activity that's great for strengthening the hand and finger muscles that little children need to hold pencils for drawing and writing.

SUN SENSE

Even young children need to understand the importance of protecting their bodies from the sun.

What You Need

- Paper • Coloured pencils and crayons
- Collection of items

What To Do

Collect some items we use to protect ourselves from the sun, such as sunglasses, hats, protective clothing, water bottle, sunscreen, beach umbrella, and so on. Next, collect some items that aren't of use.

Sit down with the children and talk to them about which items we need if we go out in the sun and why. Children need to learn from an early age about the dangers of too much sun exposure.

After you have discussed this thoroughly with the children, they could draw or list the items that protect us from the sun.

A SPINNING SWING

Make a terrific spinning swing for the garden from five motorbike tyres.

What You Need

- Five motorbike tyres (easily obtainable from tyre or bike shops) • Rope
  - A very sturdy branch in the garden with plenty of room around it

What To Do

Lash the four top tyres together standing up and then lash them very securely onto a base tyre.

Tie a double length of strong rope through the tyres and hang onto a very secure branch. You can also tie a length of rope to the side so that the swing can be pulled and spun.

The children will love climbing, swinging and spinning on their very special swing.

BEANBAG BALANCING

3

A fun game that helps develop coordination, balance and control.

What You Need

- Beanbag for balancing • Simple obstacle course
using a tyre or hoop, cardboard boxes, beach towels
or hessian bags, and a broom

What To Do

Make a simple beanbag by filling a sock with lima beans, split peas or rice. Tuck the sock inside its mate so no filling can spill out.

Let your children help you mark out the obstacle course. Together, think of different ways that the children can carry a beanbag without using their hands—on their head, under their arm, jumping with it between their legs, under their chin, between their elbows, between their wrists, and so on.

They then choose a way to carry the beanbag from the start to the first obstacle, then choose a different method to the second obstacle, and so on, until they have completed the course. If they drop the beanbag at any stage, they go back to the start of that section and try again.

Have a turn yourself—it is not as easy as it sounds!

3+

BIKE-TYRE SWINGS

Motorbike tyres can be easily obtained from tyre shops and make great swings and climbing equipment for the backyard.

What You Need

- Motorbike tyres • Strong rope
- Trees with strong limbs to which to tie the swings

What To Do

Lash two or three motorbike tyres together, one above the other with the lowest one only a small distance from the ground, and hang from a strong limb of a sturdy tree in your garden.

The children will love swinging on them and enjoy the challenge of climbing on the tyres as they move. Activities like this promote strong muscle develop and general agility.

Two children will be able to swing together, with one sitting in a low tyre and one higher up.

Hint!

If you are worried about falls, place a large foam mat or an old foam mattress under the equipment.

Sand or bark pieces also provide a good soft landing under climbing apparatus.

BLIND MAN'S BUFF

*Play this traditional children's game at a birthday party
or when you have a large group of children together.*

What You Need

• A blindfold • Children • Space to play

What To Do

Use a large clear space outdoors with no objects that the blindfolded child could trip over or walk into. Supervise carefully!

One child is chosen to be 'it' and blindfolded with a large hanky, a folded scarf or an aeroplane blindfold.

'It' is spun around a few times while the other children scatter. On the fifth spin call out 'freeze' and the other children must stay where they are.

'It' begins to search by calling out 'blind man's …' and the other players must reply 'buff'. They can try to disguise their voices.

When 'it' catches a player he must try to identify them by touch or by their voice. When correctly identified that child becomes 'it'.

3+

CONE TOSS

Many of the coastal regions of Australia are home to the beautiful Banksia Spinulosa. The dried wood cones left after it has flowered make great balls for games. Collect some from under the banksias and play games with the children next time you have a picnic at the beach.

What You Need

- Banksia cones • Room to play

What To Do

The first player tosses his cone from an official throwing spot marked by a stick or a line in the ground. The other players try to toss their banksia cones as close as possible to the first one without actually touching it.

Another game entails drawing a target on the ground with a stick and the players try to toss their banksia cones as close as possible to the target.

When lunch is over and the picnic basket is empty, use it as a target and see who can toss the most cones into the basket.

DIFFERENT BUBBLES

Encourage your children to make bubbles with non-conventional bubble-makers.

What You Need

- Detergent • Water • A little glycerine or cooking oil
- Bubble-makers such as straws, funnels, plastic spools, wire, pipe-cleaners • Clear plastic

What To Do

It's fun to make bubbles with commercial bubble-makers, but it is even more interesting to make them with a variety of things we have around the house.

Let the children help you make up the bubble mixture. Now give them a variety of materials and challenge them to use these to make great bubbles.

Don't forget to have the camera handy to record some of the beautiful bubbles they will make.

EGG CARTON CUBBIES

Make a great egg carton cubby with the children as a holiday project.

What You Need

- Lots of cardboard egg cartons • PVA glue

What To Do

Ask everyone you know to collect egg cartons. When you have enough to begin building a cubby, decide with the children how large it is going to be. Lay out the base and glue together. (This is a great activity to do outside in a covered area as egg cartons don't cope well with being wet.)

The second row is laid like bricks with each egg carton halfway across the one below. Use half egg cartons to even up the doorway. As the cubby grows higher, don't forget to leave spaces for a couple of windows. Only do a little each day as you need to let the glue dry thoroughly.

When the egg carton cubby is tall enough, make a roof from a large piece of cardboard (visit your local electrical appliance store).

The children might like to decorate their cubby with poster or acrylic paints.

They will have great fun playing pretending games in their cubby and the only cost was the glue!

FREEZE

Another good outdoor game to play with a group of children.

What You Need

- Space • A few players

What To Do

One person is 'in' and stands with his back to the other children, but a fair distance away. The other children start to move towards the person who is 'in'. Every now and then, the person who is 'in' turns around and the other children have to freeze. If any of these children are spotted moving, they are named by the person who is 'in' and must leave the game.

The first player to reach and touch the 'in' player is the winner and is 'in' for the next round.

GARDEN OBSTACLE COURSE

Make an obstacle course in the garden to help develop
your children's balance and muscle control.

What You Need

- Rope or the garden hose • Ladder
- Rebounder or old mattress • Tyres
- Cardboard boxes • Hoops
- Strong smooth boards • Broom

What To Do

With your children, set up an obstacle course in the garden. Incorporate any structures you may have, such as swings or a slide. You want your children to move in as many different ways as possible. Your children could:

Crawl under some garden chairs
Jump ten times on the rebounder or mattress
Jump through three or four tyres or hoops
Jump over the broom
Walk along the curvy rope or hose
Run around a tree
Crawl up a plank balanced on a strong box
Hop through the rungs of a ladder laid flat on the ground
Walk sideways back to the start

This game is as endless as your imagination.

HANKY TUGS

A new way to play tug-of-war.

What You Need

- Three players
- A rope tied together to make a circle
- Three hankies

What To Do

The three players hold the circle of rope and pull it tight. Make sure the children are equally spaced on the rope. Place the hankies at equal distances away from each child on the ground. When you say 'go', they must pull as hard as they can on the rope with one hand to try to reach their hanky with the other. The first person to pick up their hanky is the winner.

JUMPING ROPES

Activities like these will help improve a child's coordination and balance.

What You Need

- A length of rope • Small cushion, beanbag
  or half a sock filled with dried beans

What To Do

Tie a cushion, beanbag or filled sock to the end of the rope. Swing the rope around just above the ground (not too fast at first!). Your children jump over the rope as it comes around.

This is fun to do with a few kids or other family members. When the rope hits someone they are out and the winner is the last one left in.

244

MR BEAR

Another group game to play with a few children or at a birthday party.

What You Need

- Children • Something to be the honey pot

What To Do

The children sit down in a circle. Choose a child to have the first turn. This child is Mr Bear. Place the 'honey pot' behind his back. Mr Bear lies down and goes to sleep—you can blindfold Mr Bear if you think he might peep. The children then chant:

Isn't it funny how bears like honey!
Go to sleep, Mr Bear!

Choose a child to creep over and steal the honey pot. When the child has returned to his space in the circle and put the honey pot behind his back, he says:

Wake up, Mr Bear!

Mr Bear then has to try and guess who has the honey pot. When he has guessed, the child with the honey pot becomes the next Mr Bear.

Make some honey sandwiches after the game, and perhaps a quick Winnie-the-Pooh story might be in order.

PICK THE BERRIES

Take your children strawberry picking. It's a fun day out and you get to bring home delicious strawberries to eat.

What You Need

- Picnic lunch • Hats
  - Sunscreen
  - Water bottles

What To Do

Take your children to a strawberry-picking farm. You'll be given buckets, then you simply walk along the rows of plants picking the berries. Pick as many as you like (you don't have to fill the buckets), then head to a nearby park for a picnic lunch.

Don't forget to take hats and sunscreen.

Strawberries taste delicious served with cream and a light sprinkling of sugar.

PLANT A TIME CAPSULE

Plant a family time capsule.

What You Need

- Well-sealed container—special time-capsule containers can be bought or use a strong biscuit tin that is well sealed with insulating tape • Items you wish to store

What To Do

It is a wonderfully exciting family project to plant a time capsule in your garden.

First, do some brainstorming with the family about what to store. Think about what makes your family unique.

Perhaps you could store:

Some of the children's school work
Some drawings and other art work
Some family photos
A cassette tape with family songs and information
A videotape of a typical day in the life of your family
Some coins
Small toys
Some photos of the outside and inside of your home
Your family story

Place all the things in the time capsule, seal it up really well and bury it somewhere in your garden. Don't forget to mark the spot and also record information about where it is and when it was buried for future reference.

One day a future archaeologist might dig it up and make you all famous!

ROPE FUN

Use a length of rope to help your child develop body control and coordination.

What You Need

- A long piece of rope

What To Do

Tell your child to take off her shoes while you stretch out a long length of rope on the grass. See if your child can think of different ways to move along it.

She could try:

Walking along the rope
Walking backwards
Jumping from side to side along the rope
Doing bunny hops over the rope
Walking with one foot on either side of the rope without touching it
Hopping along the rope on one foot
Crawling along the rope
Moving along the rope using one hand and one foot

See if you can think of other ways of moving with your child. After she has tried the moves with a straight rope, have her try them on a rope that is laid in a wiggly line.

SAND COOKING

*For children, play is often a way of acting out
the social situations they encounter in real life.*

What You Need

- Cake tins • Muffin or patty cake trays
- Old frypans and saucepans • Jelly moulds
- Plastic containers • Plastic bowls
- Sieves • Ice-cube trays
- Wooden, plastic or metal spoons

What To Do

Give the children a basket of cooking implements for the sandpit. If you don't have old things to donate to the sandpit, buy some from a charity store.

Turn an old box into a stove by drawing some hotplates on the top and putting in a couple of 'trays'. Your children will 'cook' with sand and water and make the most delicious 'dinners' ever.

Make sure you leave some time in your busy day to visit and be waited on!

TEDDY BEARS' PICNIC

*Next time you and your young children are having a bad day, arrange
a teddy bears' picnic. They will be enchanted and you will be good friends again!*

What You Need

- Paper and pen
- Picnic food and drink
- Picnic rug • Soft toys

What To Do

Decide with your children which 'toy friends' they would like to invite to the picnic, then make some simple invitations together. They can decorate the invitations while you do the actual writing. Then they can be the 'postie' and deliver them.

Together, decide on the picnic fare—fruit, chunks of cheese, sausage, savoury biscuits and fairy bread make an appealing picnic lunch. Don't forget the cool drinks!

Arrange the food on a rug or tablecloth in a cool part of the garden. After you (and the toys!) have eaten, sing the teddy bears' picnic song and read some books about bears.

After the picnic is cleared away, pop your children into bed for a nap with all their cuddly friends and put your feet up. You deserve it!

THE BEANSTALK GIANT'S TREASURE

*A great chasing game to play when you have a group of children together.
If the children don't know the story of 'Jack and the Beanstalk',
tell it before the game begins.*

What You Need

- Lots of space to run • Lots of children
- A beanbag or sock filled with rice or beans

What To Do

One child is the 'giant' and sits down with his treasure behind him. The other children are all 'Jack' and have to try to steal the giant's treasure.

Designate a safe area that is home. The other children start there and try to sneak up behind the giant. If the giant hears them, they have to freeze or return to the start—home. When someone succeeds in stealing the treasure the giant has to try to catch that person before she reaches home.

If the giant doesn't catch her, a new giant is chosen. If he does, anyone who is caught joins the giant's team and becomes an assistant giant and tries to catch the Jacks.

WACKO

A fun variation on a game of skittles.

What You Need

- Empty plastic soft-drink bottles
- Sand • Chalk • Large ball

What To Do

Ask your children to pour about a cup of sand into each soft-drink bottle. This will keep the bottles from toppling over easily.

Draw a large circle on the concrete or pavers with the chalk, or make a circle on the lawn with the hose.

Place all the bottles inside the circle and take it in turns to roll a ball along the ground and see how many bottles you can knock out of the circle.

Use this activity as a counting game as well. Your children can keep the scores on paper or their blackboard.

WASHING THE DOLLS' CLOTHES

Any activity that involves water is always popular with young children.

What You Need

- A large plastic washing-up dish • Water • Laundry detergent
- A child's clothesline or a fold-up clothes drier • Pegs
- A child's laundry trolley or small basket
- Dolls and dolls' clothes to wash

What To Do

On a sunny day your children will love washing their dolls and their dolls' clothes outside in the garden. Children love play that involves acting out real-life experiences and washing is certainly one of those!

Also, using pegs helps develop those finger and hand muscles that young children need to use for drawing and writing.

WATER SLIDES

If you have a grassy slope in your garden, turn it into an exciting water slide.

What You Need

- Plastic sheeting or large strong plastic garbage bags
- Plastic tent pegs • Sprinkler or hose

What To Do

Use the plastic tent pegs to secure the plastic sheeting on a grassy incline in your garden. Set up the sprinkler or hose so the water runs down the plastic. Step back and watch the kids as they splash and slide!

If you add a little detergent to the slide, it will increase the slipperiness, but warn the children first. Don't forget to apply lots of sunscreen and to supervise this activity closely.

COLOUR TRAIL

Help your children learn their colours by making a colour trail.

What You Need

- Simple different-coloured objects

What To Do

Lay a trail in your backyard using different-coloured objects from around the house. Tell your children to follow the trail and collect only the objects of one colour, such as red.

For variety, ask your children to make a trail using objects of just one colour. Make sure they don't use anything precious that might break!

DOGGY, WHERE'S YOUR BONE?

A game that children of all ages love to play.

What You Need

- Children • A 'bone' cut out of a plastic
ice-cream lid or from cardboard • Blindfold

What To Do

The children sit down in a circle and join hands. Choose a child to have the first turn. This child sits in the middle of the circle, wearing the blindfold, and with the 'bone' behind her back.

Choose another child from the circle to creep out and steal the doggy's bone and hide it behind his back.

Everyone then chants:

Doggy, doggy, where's your bone?
Somebody stole it from your home.
Who stole the bone?

The child who stole the bone replies:

I stole the bone.

The blindfolded child then has to guess who has the bone. The game is harder if you encourage the children not to tell who has the bone, and not to giggle if they have it, and if everyone puts their hands behind their back—not just the person with the bone.

FUNNEL PHONES

Make a simple phone to play with in the backyard with the children.

What You Need

- Plastic funnels • A length of clear plastic tubing with a diameter the same size as the funnel nozzle

What To Do

You can buy clear plastic tubing from your local hardware store. Buy enough to enable the children to take their phones around corners, so they can be out of sight when they talk to each other. The hardware staff will help you match the tubing to the funnels.

At home, fit the ends of the tubing to the funnels. If it is a very tight squeeze, dip the ends into boiling water and then squeeze the funnel nozzles into the softened tubing.

Take the contraption out in the garden with the children. They will love talking to you and to each other on their 'funnel phone'.

When they have tired of this new toy, cut the tubing into lengths and give it to them to use for pouring and measuring in the bath or in the backyard wading pool.

GOLF-BALL FUN

*If you are not golfers, collect some old golf balls from golfing friends.
Your children will love using them in the sandpit or at the beach.*

What You Need

- Sand • Golf balls

What To Do

My son loves to make sandcastles in the sandpit, and then make tunnels and tracks to roll golf balls down. They work better than other balls because they are small and heavy, but you must supervise well as these hard balls can cause real damage if thrown.

The sand needs to be damp for this activity.

Build a large sandcastle with the children and then use a golf ball to make a track around the castle from top to bottom. You could even make tunnels for the golf balls to run through. Do test runs as you work because the tracks may need higher edges so the balls don't run off.

Talk to the children as you work together and encourage them to try to think of solutions to problems as they occur. They will have lots of fun racing their golf balls down their tracks. If it is a nice warm day let them use the hose in the sandpit as it is great fun if the golf balls roll down and splash into a puddle of water!

HOPSCOTCH

After your children have mastered jumpscotch (see p227),
playing hopscotch will further develop their coordination and balance,
and also help them learn numbers in a fun way.

What You Need

• Chalk • Stones or small beanbags

What To Do

Mark out a traditional hopscotch pattern on some concrete or pavers. Perhaps you and your children can come up with some new patterns of your own, maybe a rocketship hopscotch game?

Explain the rules of hopscotch to them. Throw the stone into section 1, jump over it and then hop in all sections up to 10. Do a jump-turn on 10, hop back again and then, while balancing on one leg in section 2, retrieve the stone. Next time, throw into section 2, then hop over that and so on. If one child throws a stone into the wrong section, it is the next player's turn.

Each player must remember which number they are up to for their next turn. Younger children can play by jumping rather than hopping on one leg.

KNOCK 'EMS

Develop your children's throwing skills with this game.

What You Need

- Six tins with lids (powdered milk or baby formula tins are ideal)
- Sand or dirt • Tape • Paint or collage materials • Balls or beanbags

What To Do

Put some sand or dirt in the tins so they don't topple over too easily. Replace the lids and tape closed.

Paint or decorate the tins with your children. Show them how to arrange the tins in a pyramid.

Have each child throw a ball or beanbag at the tins. Count how many tins are knocked over. Keep score (this is good counting practice!).

MAKE A TEPEE

Children still love playing Cowboys and Indians just as we did when we were young. Of course a few props really help!

What You Need

- A large piece of hessian 2 m x 4 m (6.5 ft x 13 ft)
- Calico for casing • Four broomsticks

What To Do

Cut the calico into two-metre-long strips, make sure they're wide enough to slip the broom handles through. Sew the casings onto one side of the hessian, spacing them evenly across the width, leaving about half a metre at each end to hang over the entrance to the tepee. Sew a hem on the top, bottom and sides of the tepee so the hessian doesn't fray.

Slip the broom handles into the casings. Stand the tepee up with the broom handles apart at the bottom, and leaning in and supporting each other at the top to give the tepee shape.

Older children will enjoy decorating the tepee with natural colours. Take them to the library to do some research on the American Indians and their art. Younger children will enjoy collecting feathers to make Indian headbands and will love playing in their new cubby.

When they have finished playing for the day, simply roll up the cubby and store it away in the garage or shed for another day.

MULTI-TYRE SWINGS

*Old tyres are cheap and easily obtainable, and can make
terrific outdoor equipment for the children to play on.*

What You Need

- Four standard car tyres • A few metres of strong rope
(rope can be bought by the metre from hardware,
camping or boating stores) • Strong trees

What To Do

Thread the tyres onto the rope. Secure the rope between two strong trees at a height that allows the children to be able to climb into and onto the tyres without adult assistance.

The children will enjoy swinging inside the tyres, climbing and holding onto them and sitting on the top.

It's also fun for them to lie in the tyres as an adult or older child pushes the tyres gently.

You will be amazed at the imaginative ways children play with such a simple piece of equipment—it will be everything from a spaceship to a submarine. In our high-tech society, our kids need simple, open-ended play equipment!

MURDER IN THE DARK

A great game to play with the children on a summer's night!

What You Need

- Children • A dark night • Torch

What To Do

One child is chosen to be the 'murderer' and counts to 100 while the others go and hide. The murderer then hunts down his victims using the torch. As they are caught they join him in the hunt. The last child to be caught becomes the next murderer.

PARACHUTE FUN

You can hire parachutes from your State Recreation Council, local toy library or from a school or pre-school. They are great to have for birthday parties or any other occasion when you have a group of children together.

What You Need
- A parachute • Soft ball

What To Do

Spread out the parachute on the ground and space the children evenly around the outside. Show them how to pick up the parachute and to hold onto it firmly.

Begin by simply lifting the parachute up and down in waves around the circle, until all the children feel comfortable holding it.

Next you can throw a large soft ball into the middle and have everyone wave the parachute up and down to stop the ball coming out of the parachute. If it does jump out, someone has to run and retrieve it and throw it back in.

Another fun activity is for everyone to lift the parachute up as high as they can and then you call out the names of a few of the children. They run under the parachute and out the other side before it is dropped down.

You can also choose some children to go under the parachute while it is lifted up and then drop it down on them. The children stand in the middle and lift up the parachute from underneath to form a tent. They will have to stand on their tiptoes and lift up their arms.

PIPES IN THE SANDPIT

4

*Add to the children's fun in the sandpit with some 'real'
equipment and they will enjoy playing 'plumbers'.*

What You Need

- PVC pipes (plumbing outlets will often let you have offcuts
  or you can buy some short lengths cheaply)
- Add some half pipes and an assortment of different joining pieces
- Provide a variety of pipes of different sizes • Hose

What To Do

On nice warm days the children will love being 'plumbers' in the sandpit with the hose and lots of different-sized pipes.

They will also enjoy laying half pipes out on the lawn and watching the water flow through them. Show them how to float some small leaf 'boats' and how to join different lengths of pipes together with joining pieces.

Next time the children see a house being built, they will be really interested in the way the pipes are being laid.

SACK RACES

I remember sack races from school sports days and Sunday School picnics, and they were always lots of fun. Try one when the children are bored or when you have a birthday party.

What You Need

- Pillowcases or polystyrene sacks
(available from fruit shops or produce agencies)

What To Do

Make out a starting and a finishing line. Give each player a sack. They get into it feet first and line up. The aim of the game is to jump, holding the sides of the sack up, to the finishing line.

Of course, it is much harder than it sounds and there will be many tumbles and lots of laughter.

SHIP TO SHORE

Another great group game to play with the children.

What You Need

- Space to run • Children

What To Do

Designate an area to be the 'ship' and one to be the 'shore'. The command 'four' means to stand in the middle and 'zed' means to sit down wherever you are. Someone is chosen to call the commands. This is the 'captain'. The players have to run as fast as they can to an area when the captain calls. The last to react to the command each time steps out and joins the captain. The last player in is the winner and becomes the next captain.

4+

TARGET PRACTICE

*Make some targets in the garden with your children
and help improve their throwing skills.*

What You Need

- Wire coat-hanger or a child's plastic hoop
  - String • Balls or beanbags

What To Do

Pull the coat-hanger into a round shape (or use a hoop) and lash it to a tree or the clothes line to make a stable target.

Your children will have lots of fun throwing balls or beanbags through the target.

To make it more interesting, tie balloons on strings or junk threadings to the target so them move when the children score a 'hit'.

As their aim improves, make them stand further away from the target to increase the challenge.

TEPEES AND INDIANS

*A lively game to play at a birthday party
or whenever you have a group of children together.*

What You Need

- Children • Space to run

What To Do

Divide the children into pairs. If there is a child left out he can be the caller for the game—emphasise that this is a very important job. In each pair, there must be an 'Indian' and a 'tepee'.

The tepee stands with his legs wide apart and his hands above his head, palms together and fingers pointing up like a tepee. The Indian sits in front of the tepee with her legs and arms crossed.

The caller then calls 'Indians' or 'tepees'. When he calls 'Indians', the Indians have to crawl through their tepee's legs and sit still with their arms and legs crossed. The last Indian back in position is out, and he and his tepee partner are out of the game.

When the caller says 'tepees', the tepees run clockwise around the circle back to their place and resume their position with their legs wide apart and their hands stretched up together like the top of a tepee. Again the last tepee in place has to leave the game with his partner. The game continues until you have a tepee and Indian pair of winners.

WASHING THE CAR

It's great to have a shiny, clean car—and the kids love helping to wash it!

What You Need

- Buckets • Sponges, rags, or chamois
- Car washing liquid • The hose

What To Do

Most children love helping to wash the car—especially if they do it on a warm day when they can wear their swimming costumes and get wet. If the children are trying to avoid this task, however, turn it into a game that's fun for everyone.

Assign each child a specific part of the car to wash—the number plates, hub-caps, bonnet, doors, and so on.

Give each child a bucket and cloth and when you say 'go' they clean their section as fast as they can. Of course, Mum or Dad will have to inspect the job to make sure that fast doesn't mean dirty!

WHAT'S THE TIME, MR WOLF?

4+

A great party game.

What You Need

- Lots of space • Lots of players

What To Do

One child is Mr Wolf and stands a fair distance away with his back to the other children. The other children hold hands and advance in a line, step by step, as they chant, 'What's the time, Mr Wolf?' They then stop walking. After each question Mr Wolf turns around and says a time, e.g. 'Seven o'clock'. Finally, when they are very close, Mr Wolf turns and says 'Dinner time!'

The children turn and run away as fast as they can with Mr Wolf chasing them. When someone is caught, they are the next Mr Wolf.

EXPLORE THE ENVIRONMENT

BIRD BATHS IN YOUR GARDEN

Birds need a regular water supply if you want to attract them to your garden.

What You Need

- A large clay pot or clay pipe at least 8 cm (3 in) high
- A large, deep clay saucer

What To Do

Visit your local nursery or pot shop with the children to buy a large clay pot and deep saucer. (A 'seconds' pot is fine for this purpose as it is only to support the saucer.) If you decide to use a clay pipe you will need to visit a plumber's supply or hardware store.

Find a suitable place in the garden where a tree can overhang the bird bath so birds can quickly fly into the tree to escape a cat. Wet feathers will hamper their ability to fly and they won't use your bird bath if they don't feel safe. (If you have a pet cat make sure it has a few bells attached to its collar to warn birds.)

Place the saucer on top of the upturned pot and make sure it is as stable as possible. Fill regularly with fresh water for the birds to drink and to use for bathing.

It will often take birds some time to find a new source of water and you can help by hanging the hose from a branch above and letting it drip slowly into your bird bath. Birds will be attracted by the splashing sound and by the pattern of ripples, and the children will soon be delighted by the birds using the bird bath.

BIRTHDAY GARDENS

*Celebrate your children's birthdays by adding a special
plant each year to their very own 'birthday garden'.*

What You Need

- A place for each child's 'birthday garden'
- A plant for each birthday • Gardening tools
- A sign for each child's garden

What To Do

When you children are born, designate a special space in your garden for each child's 'birthday garden'. Celebrate each birthday by putting a special plant in their garden. As your children grow older they will look forward to this special event and enjoy going with you to the nursery to choose their special birthday plant.

Make a special sign for their garden and encourage them to help you care for their special place.

This becomes a lovely family tradition and is a great way to introduce children to the pleasures of gardening.

PARKS

*Do you use your local parks? Do you regularly
take your children to parks or are they just
something green to admire from the car as
you drive past? Make the effort to use your local
parks and enjoy some special times with your family.*

What You Need

• A park • Time

What To Do

It is great if you can walk to your local park, but if not, pack up the car or even ride your bike there with the children. No matter how you get there, do it regularly because as ratepayers we should all be using them more.

The children will enjoy the play equipment. If it's not exciting and challenging, join with other parents to lobby your local council to upgrade it. Take the children's balls, bikes, rollerblades and kites and use them in the safe environment of the park—you'll have lots more room to play than in your backyard.

Meet friends there. If there are barbecue facilities, have a sausage sizzle for lunch.

PET RESPECT

It's very important that children learn respect for other creatures at an early age. This can start right at home with your family pets.

What You Need

- A pet • Time

What To Do

When children are very young, they do not understand that if they pull a dog's tail or a cat's fur, they will hurt them.

Teaching your children to respect pets from an early age not only makes life more comfortable for your pet, but it teaches your children respect for others. There is also a safety aspect to this lesson—if your children pull the tail of a unfriendly cat or dog, they may get a bite or a scratch!

Show your children how to care for the family pet. Let little ones brush Fido or Fluffy, under your supervision. Let them help out at feeding time. Let them come with you when you take Fido for his daily walk.

Small birds such as budgies also make good pets for young children. Children will delight in trying to teach a bird to talk, or feeding it.

Who knows—you may have a future vet in the family!

WATERING CANS

Buy a watering can so your littlies can help in the garden, too.

What You Need

- A watering can

What To Do

Young children love to be involved in our activities. When he was two, our son was given a gardening set as a Christmas gift by my sister Julie. It was one of the best presents he has ever had.

He still follows me around with the wheelbarrow when I'm weeding and loves to help pick up the weeds. The small rake has broken, but I've cut down the handle of an adult-sized one and he enjoys helping with the raking, but the most popular item has always been the watering can.

Children of all ages love playing with water, and letting them water the garden encourages a water activity that has a useful purpose. By giving them simple tasks, you are building their self-esteem and independence skills.

ZOO ANIMALS

Children are fascinated by animals and even the youngest child will enjoy a trip to the zoo. Introduce your children to the zoo from an early age. They will love it!

What You Need

- Zoo • Pencils
- Paper • Time

What To Do

Visit a zoo nearest you. Younger children will enjoy the larger, more active animals, while older children will be fascinated with butterflies, snakes and frogs. Sit back and enjoy your children's wonder at the beautiful creatures we share this planet with.

When you get home, reinforce what the children have learned on their trip to the zoo with follow-up activities. Focus on picture books about zoo animals with younger children. Pre-schoolers will enjoy drawing and painting what they saw, also.

BUBBLES

*Bubbles are great fun to make on a windy day. Your children
can work out which direction the wind is coming from.*

What You Need

- Detergent • Water • Container
  - Cooking oil or glycerine
    - Bubble-makers

What To Do

Make up a strong solution of bubble mixture with washing-up detergent and water. A teaspoon of cooking oil or glycerine added to the mixture makes the bubbles stronger.

Give your children bubble-makers—large ones to make gigantic bubbles can often be bought at flea markets and provide hours of fun.

Make bubbles together and watch them float. See whose bubbles go the highest and drift the furthest. Young children love chasing the bubbles you make, too!

FOOTPRINT SPOTTING

Play detectives in the sand and spot footprints with the children at the beach.

What You Need

- The beach • Children

What To Do

When you go for walks on the beach with the children it is fun to look for and even track different footprints in the sand. See if the children can discover different types of shoes, bird prints, dog prints and different-sized footprints.

When you turn round, see if you can follow your own family's prints back to where you began. If the sea has come in and covered them, explain tides to the children.

GARDEN DETECTIVES

Encourage your children's thinking and questioning skills with this fun activity.

What You Need

• Time

What To Do

Play a guessing game in the garden with the children. Tell them you are thinking of something that they can all see. Provide a few clues, and then it is up to them to ask questions until they get the answer.

Younger children may need more help, so start with a couple of clues and they will ask for more.

This game can be played in the car, at the beach, or anywhere with any number of children. The child who guesses correctly has the next turn to think of an item.

INSECT HUNT

Keeping insects will help your children find out more about them and foster an interest in nature.

What You Need

- Any small box, but a shoebox is ideal
- Piece of net • Large rubber band or piece of elastic

What To Do

Go with your children on a 'bug' hunt. Take a bottle, a fine net or a bug catcher to trap them. Put your bug in a box and cover the top with netting (secure it with a rubber band). Make sure you collect some of the leaves you trap your bug on to put in the bug box with it.

Make sure your children understand that we only keep insects and other creatures twenty minutes or so, after which they must be returned to their 'families'.

INVESTIGATING ROCK POOLS

2+

*Next time you visit a beach which has a rocky headland,
spend some time with the kids investigating the rock pools.*

What You Need
- Time

What To Do

Take the children to the beach and spend some time investigating the amazing life in rock pools. Many rocks which are covered by high tides are very slippery, so make sure everyone wears shoes that have good flexible soles. Warn the children not to walk on rocks that are green or look slimy.

Find some rock pools that are covered at high tide. See if the children can spot small fish, crabs, sea anemones, mussels and other living things amidst the rocks and sea weed. Last year on holidays in northern New South Wales we found many starfish in beautiful clear rock pools.

Sometimes you may have to help the children carefully lift up a few rocks to see what is hidden under them.

My son loves to place his finger carefully into anemones to feel them pull shut and try to suck in the finger. This helps him understand how the anemone catches its prey.

See if you and the children can count how many different animals you can find in the rock pools.

PLANT A ROSE GARDEN OF MEMORIES

Roses are such special plants and nothing looks or smells nicer in the house than a bowl of roses. Plant a rose garden with your family to celebrate special events.

What You Need

- Rose bushes • Gardening tools

What To Do

Consider planting a Memorial Rose Garden in your garden. You could plant a rose bush for family births and deaths, for special occasions such as wedding anniversaries or children's birthdays, or to commemorate special events such as school graduations or excellent examination results, and so on.

There are many wonderful rose varieties available, and roses come in bushes, climbers, ground covers and miniature rose bushes.

You could also plant varieties with names that match the special event or person, or rename the bushes and add metal tags with names and dates so you know why and when they were planted.

The children will enjoy helping to care for their special roses.

SAND WALLS

Sometimes, very young children are a little nervous of the sea and the waves on their first few visits to the beach. Help your children overcome any fears with this great activity at the water's edge.

What You Need

- Buckets and spades • Time

What To Do

Choose a day when the surf is not too rough and pick a time when you can see the tide is coming in. Several metres below high-water mark (but far enough from the water to allow you time to do this activity!) help your children build a thick sand wall, to keep the tide back. Make it a family effort, with everyone from oldest to youngest working to pile sand about a half a metre high and wide.

Because you are close to the water as you are all working, youngsters will soon lose their fear of the approaching tide and happily throw themselves into building the wall.

Once your sand wall is finished, you can all retreat to a higher part of the beach and enjoy a family picnic, while you wait to see how long your sand wall stands up against the waves!

Important!

Always remember that children should be closely supervised at all times, whenever they are near water.

SEED SORTING

Sorting and matching are important mathematical skills.

What You Need

- A mixture of seeds
- A muffin tin or an egg carton

What To Do

Buy a few packets of seeds or use a bag of soup mix. Show your children how to sort the seeds into different categories, but encourage them to think of their own sorting criteria.

The children can put the different categories of seeds into the holes in the muffin tin or egg carton. When they have finished sorting, talk to them about what they did and why. See if they can count each pile to see which one has the most seeds.

Plant a selection of the seeds in a pot or in the garden so your children can enjoy watching their seeds grow.

SPACESHIP TO THE MOON

Children love to play with cardboard boxes—whether they are making cubby houses in them, or flying imaginary spaceships to the moon. Help your children to create their very own spaceship out of a simple cardboard box.

What You Need

- Large cardboard boxes, big enough for the children to sit in
- Pencil • Non-toxic powder paints • Brushes

What To Do

Talk to your children about the moon, and explain that astronauts have walked on the moon. Show your children photographs of the moon, then ask your children if they want to make their very own spaceships and pretend to travel to the moon.

Give your children a cardboard box each and have them spend a few minutes thinking about what sort of a spaceship they might like. How many rockets does it have? Does it have windows? Older children will come up with all sorts of interesting ideas.

Using the pencil, help your children to draw features onto the boxes. Then let them loose outside with several different-coloured paints to create their dream machine.

Allow several hours for the paint to dry thoroughly before your children bring their spaceships inside. They'll have hours of fun going on imaginary trips to the moon in their new spaceships.

ANT WATCHING

Help your children learn about their environment by watching ants.

What You Need

- An ants' nest • Magnifying glass
- Time • Small crumbs of food

What To Do

In the garden or in a park find an ants' nest with the children. Ants build a small mound from dirt or sand that is easy to spot.

Feed the ants tiny crumbs of bread or other food and then watch to see what happens.

Ants will carry really large loads back into the nest. Take along a magnifying glass so the children can observe the ants closely.

BUDGERIGARS

Budgies are one of the most popular family pets. If your children want a pet of their own, consider getting them a couple of budgies.

What You Need

- A large cage or aviary
- Two budgerigars

What To Do

Visit your local pet shop with the children so they can choose their own birds. Young birds are best, and encourage the children to choose budgies that have different-coloured plumage for easier identification.

Because budgies are gregarious, they should be kept in pairs, and you should make sure their cage is large enough to allow them to fly a little. Their cage should also contain a few perches, a bell, bath, mirror and swing, together with seed and water dispensers that cannot be contaminated by droppings.

Budgies are seed-eaters and their seed needs to be topped up daily. Most commercial budgie seed mixtures are excellent, but the children will enjoy supplementing the birds' diet with pieces of vegetables, fruit, and seeded grasses from the garden. My budgies have always enjoyed eating soft thistles, too.

Cover the bottom of their cage or aviary with grit as they need this to help digestion and for trimming their beaks.

If you keep their wings trimmed, you can let your budgies out for a little gentle play. If the children want to handle the birds, teach them to hold the birds gently in their cupped hands.

COMPOSTING

*Teach your children about the environment in
your own garden by making compost together.*

What You Need

- Kitchen scrap bin
- Compost bin • Soil
- Animal manure

What To Do

The soil in your garden is like every other living thing—it needs nourishment. Take your children for a walk through a bush area or a rainforest and look at the amount of leaf and other litter on the forest floor. Talk to the children about the value of this natural recycling and about how we can replicate this important process in our own gardens.

We have a small plastic bucket beside our sink in the kitchen in which we store our compost materials. Your children can learn to add their apple cores, fruit peelings, and so on to the compost bucket, and be responsible for emptying it every couple of days.

We have a large black compost bin and this works very well. If you can't afford a compost bin, make an area for a compost heap in your garden. Buy some heavy-duty black plastic to cover the heap as this will warm it and help to break it down more quickly. Keep the plastic in place with bricks.

Every few weeks add a layer of garden soil, together with horse, cow, chicken or sheep manure to your compost bin and keep it moist. In time the compost will change into a wonderful rich fertiliser you can feed your plants.

DECIDUOUS TREES

*Plant a deciduous tree in your garden with the children
so the whole family can enjoy the beauty of autumn.*

What You Need

- A seedling from a local nursery
- Gardening tools

What To Do

Autumn is such a special time of year. The days become shorter and there's a touch of crispness in the air. There are also trees such as liquidambars which colour beautifully and lose their leaves. Many beautiful deciduous trees develop wonderful colours in autumn such as the maples, birches, linden trees and a large variety of Japanese maples.

The children will love helping you choose a deciduous tree for your garden and the whole family will enjoy its colourful beauty in autumn time.

FLOATING AND SINKING

Children learn best by doing things themselves.

What You Need

- A selection of household objects that float and sink, such as plastic, paper, toys, corks, feathers, pegs, foam, ping-pong balls, a golf ball, wood, containers with holes • A large dish of water

What To Do

This is a great activity to do outside on a warm day. Give the children some of the household items listed above. The children will love seeing which objects float and which sink in the large dish of water. They can sort the objects into the two categories. (Sorting is also an important numeracy skill.)

See if they can make changes to some of the objects that float to make them sink, and vice versa. Encourage them to talk about what they are seeing.

Older children who can write may like to write a piece about this activity to take to school for a class talk.

FRAGRANT SHOEBOX

See how well your children can distinguish different smells with this fun activity.

What You Need

- Aromatic substances, such as chocolate, lavender,
  lemon peel, onion, orange peel, peanut paste,
  perfume, soap, vanilla essence, Vegemite
- Shoebox • Rubber bands • Drinking straws
- Paper • Plastic bags • Coloured felt pens

What To Do

Punch six holes for the drinking straws at intervals in the lid of the box. Put six smelling substances in plastic bags and attach the straws to the bags with rubber bands. Place the bags in the box and put the straws through the holes. Colour some small pieces of paper the colour of each substance, e.g. light brown for peanut paste, yellow for lemon peel, to give clues and help discussion about the scents.

Let your children smell the different scents and then talk together about what they think they are, or what they remind them of.

Happy sniffing!

GOLDFISH

When your children want a pet of their own consider buying a couple of goldfish.
They are easy to look after and are very relaxing to watch.

What You Need

- A fish tank or bowl • Fish food
- Washed river sand or washed pebbles
- Water plants • Water neutraliser

What To Do

Goldfish do not need a heater or bubbler in their tank, so they are much easier to care for than tropical fish. The sales assistant in the pet shop will advise you about the size of bowl or tank you will need for the number of fish you are buying.

Set up the tank at least two days before you buy the goldfish. Add water weeds—very important as they produce oxygen and help purify the water. Add water snails too—they help clean the tank. Don't use shells for decoration as the lime content in shells can make your goldfish ill.

Let your children choose their fish, which will be given to you in a bag of water. Leave the bag to float in your own tank at home for at least ten minutes so the fish become accustomed to the water temperature of your tank.

Remind your children that fish must not be over-fed, and tell them also that goldfish have a special coating of mucus to keep them healthy and this can be damaged if touched.

GRASS HEADS

While these can be bought from many craft markets, they are simple and fun to make with your children.

What You Need

- Old pantihose or stockings • Scissors
- Plastic container, such as margarine, yoghurt
- Grass seeds • Tablespoon
- Potting mix
- Stickers or felt pens

What To Do

Cut off one leg of the pantihose and hold it open while your children spoon in at least three tablespoons of grass seeds. Then add three to four cups of potting mix. Knot the stocking securely above the potting mix and shape it into a round 'head'. Place it in the container.

Your children will enjoy making a face on the grass head and perhaps adding decorative touches to the container, such as a tie and buttons.

Keep the grass head damp, and in a few days it will begin to grow a lovely head of bright green hair.

GROW A PINEAPPLE PLANT

Last year ,while on holidays on Queensland's lovely Sunshine Coast,
we visited the Big Pineapple and my son came home really wanting
to grow a pineapple plant after seeing how to do it on the train tour.
Try growing one with your own children. It's easy.

What You Need

- A pineapple with the top still on
- Gardening tools

What To Do

Chop off the top of the plant and eat the delicious sweet pineapple with the children.

Leave the top in the garden for a few weeks so it dies out really well. The farmers at the Big Pineapple do this so the plant doesn't develop rot and die.

In a few weeks the top will be ready to plant in a sunny spot in the garden or in a well-drained pot. In time, if you live in a warm enough climate, your pineapple plant will grow a new pineapple. If it doesn't, it is still an interesting and decorative plant.

Did you know that each successive pineapple on a plant will be smaller? Most farmers only grow two pineapples from a plant as the fruit becomes too small to market commercially. There are two sorts of pineapples—roughs and smooths. Although we usually buy smooths in the shops, the roughs are more delicious and taste really sweet!

GROWING BULBS

Nothing heralds spring as much as a pot of beautiful flowering bulbs.

What You Need

- Pretty pots • Bulb potting mix
- Bulbs • Gardening tools

What To Do

Bulbs are self-contained seeds and little energy houses. Plant some with your children, and watch the bulbs as the temperature warms up. The hard, dried-up looking bulbs begin growing and burst out with lovely new green shoots and eventually beautiful flowers.

Choose firm round bulbs that have been properly dried out. Buy some special bulb-raising potting mix or bulb fibre. Help the children add about 2.5 cm (1 in) of potting mix or fibre to a shallow pot, then add 4–6 bulbs. Pack the rest of the pot with more potting mix or bulb fibre until the tops of the bulbs are covered.

The bulbs should be allowed to start growing in the dark and then moved out to a shaded window ledge or a spot in the garden as soon as they begin to grow. Water sparingly, bulbs are likely to rot if the conditions are too damp.

Everyone has their own favourite bulbs, but I always think daffodils and jonquils say spring to me with their beautiful flowers and wonderful perfumes. But then hyacinths are so beautiful too! And freesias smell so divine! The hardest part about growing bulbs with the children is choosing which ones to grow.

LEAF HUNT

A matching game to play in your garden that will
encourage an interest in plants and trees.

What You Need

- Leaves from plants in your garden
  - Paper • Pencils or crayons

What To Do

Collect a variety of leaves from different plants in the garden and show them to your children.

Then go for a walk around the garden with your children and see if they can match the leaves to the plant they come from. (If you don't have a garden, do it in a local park.)

Later, your children can try leaf rubbings. Place the leaf with the vein-side up on a piece of paper. Put a piece of paper over the leaf. Hold it very still and rub over the paper with the side of a pencil or crayon. You will see the leaf shape, veins and stem clearly on the rubbing.

MORE ABOUT GOLDFISH

*If your children have goldfish, encourage them to find
out a little more about their special pets.*

What You Need

- A library

What To Do

Encourage your children to observe their goldfish. Borrow books from the library to help your
children discover facts like:

Goldfish don't sleep like humans do
Goldfish can't close their eyes
They have a rest by not swimming
They seem to like each other's company
They use their tails to help them swim

If you can remember any old goldfish songs such as '1, 2, 3, 4, 5' share them with your children.
See if you can remember the finger plays from your own childhood.

1, 2, 3, 4, 5,
Once I caught a fish alive.
6, 7, 8, 9, 10,
Then I let him go again.
Why did you let him go?
Because he bit my finger so.
Which finger did he bite?
This little finger on the right.

PLANT A TREE

*Help your children develop a love of gardening and the
environment with this long-term project.*

What You Need

- A small tree to plant
- Gardening books or magazines
- Your camera • A notebook

What To Do

Look through gardening magazines and books (borrow some from your local library if you do not
have them at home) to find a tree suitable for your climate and type of garden.

Take your children to the nursery with you to choose the tree. At home, help them plant it and
make them responsible for its care.

Don't forget to take photos of them planting and caring for their tree. Take annual photos of the
children with the tree and use them in a tree diary. It's fascinating to note how much the children
and tree have grown!

In their tree diary, they can also:

Do rubbings of the tree's bark
Press the tree's flowers
Record the tree's height and girth
Do leaf rubbings of the leaves

RIVERS IN THE SANDPIT

*On hot days the hose in the sandpit is most children's idea of heaven.
Turn a blind eye to the mess and the wet clothes and help turn it into
a great geography lesson.*

What You Need

- Sandpit • Hose

What To Do

Join your children in the sandpit and bring the hose. Suggest you make a little creek together. Dig out the creek and let the hose run into it—soon there will be billabongs, waterfalls, lakes and, eventually, a big river. Explain and name these features and compare them to real ones you have seen together. When it becomes too wet, turn off the hose, have a picnic and then watch as the 'drought' dries up all the water.

Next time you go for a drive in the country together, look for the geographical features that you made together in the sandpit.

TIME CLOCKS

Help young children learn about time by making some fun cardboard clocks that can be positioned to show different times, such as breakfast, lunch and dinnertime, or time for playgroup!

What You Need

- Sheets of thin cardboard, around 45 cm (18 in) square
- Smaller pieces of cardboard for the clock hands
- Marker pens • Scissors • Paper fasteners • Blu-Tack

What To Do

Together with your children, decide on how many clocks you are going to make. You may want a clock in the kitchen for meal times, a clock in the bathroom for bath time and a clock in their bedroom for bedtime.

Next, use the base of a round pan from the kitchen to draw a circle on each piece of cardboard. Then draw the clock numbers around the circles, using bright marker pens. Cut out pairs of hands for the clocks and fasten them to the clock faces with the paper fasteners. Your children can decorate the outer edges of each clock with a few small drawings of their own that relate to the time of day that clock represents.

Hang the clocks in different spots, using Blu-Tack. The children will enjoy looking at their clocks and learning about the time from their very own creations.

TORCH GAMES

*A torch makes a great gift for a young child. Having a torch close
at hand can make a child feel more secure in a dark bedroom.*

What You Need

- A torch with batteries

What To Do

Your child can help you go on a 'treasure hunt' to collect lots of items made of different materials.
Collect objects made of wood, plastic, paper, metal, china and fabric.

Take the objects outside when it's really dark, or take them into a dark room.

Your child then turns on his torch and works out which objects are shiny and which are dull. He will
also enjoy finding out which objects the torchlight will shine through and which objects are opaque.

Torches are great for shadow games, too. Perhaps one warm night you could go for a walk
together and look for 'spooky' shapes and then find out what they really are!

WATCHING DRAGONFLIES

Visit a pond or other swampy area and watch
some fascinating dragonflies with your children.

What You Need

• Time • An insect net • Glass jar

What To Do

There are thousands of different dragonfly species in the world. They live near water, usually slow-moving water, such as dams, ponds, marshes or stagnant creeks. Visit an area like this with your children and introduce them to the dainty, beautiful dragonfly.

Take an insect or butterfly net with you and see if you can catch one for the children to have a closer look. Carefully put it into a glass jar. Take care not to damage its delicate wings.

Point out its enormous compound eyes, which cover almost all of the dragonfly's head and give it incredibly wide vision. Explain to the children that dragonflies hatch out of eggs, and the nymphs have gills and live in water. When a nymph is ready to change into a dragonfly, it climbs out of the water and the change occurs.

Make sure you return your dragonfly to its environment before you leave, so it can enjoy the rest of its very short life.

WET WASHING

*Make washing day fun by using this household chore as
an opportunity to teach your children about wind power.*

What You Need

- Washing line
- Wet washing

What To Do

Younger children are fascinated by the wind and love to see objects such as windmills at work.
Explain to your children that when you hang wet clothes outside on a windy day, they dry quicker.
The wind blows on the clothes, drying them out. The windier the day, the faster the clothes will
dry! These facts seem obvious to an adult but they are new and interesting to young children.

Have your children help you hang the washing out on a windy day. Point out how the wind makes
the clothes flap about. Then teach them this old favourite:

Wet, wet washing hanging on the line,
When the weather's fine.
Along comes the wind
and blows it all around.
Flip-flap, flip-flap,
When the weather's fine.

At 'blows it all around', have your children join you in spinning around with their arms
outstretched. Fun for everyone!

WINDMILLS

*On a windy day, it's fun to make coloured
windmills and watch them spin in the wind.*

What You Need

- Coloured paper • Scissors
- Ruler • Pencil • Pins
- Drinking straws or small sticks

What To Do

Draw up squares on some coloured paper for the children to cut out. Talk about what makes a
square different from a rectangle while they are cutting. Next, help them draw four lines with
a ruler from each corner to near the middle of each square (see the illustration below).

Bring the outside of each triangle into the middle and secure with a pin or drawing pin poked into
the drinking straw.

Take the windmills outside and hold them in the wind, and watch how fast they fly!

BALLOON MYSTERIES

Do your children ask you lots of difficult-to-answer questions such as, 'Why do balloons bounce?' Try this simple experiment together to discover why balloons do bounce.

What You Need

- Balloons

What To Do

Blow up a balloon for each child and tie it so the air will not escape. Tell your children to push down as hard as they can on their balloons and bounce them against different surfaces.

What happens when they push their balloon down hard? Explain that when you blow air into balloons the air molecules are very tightly packed together. By pushing down on the balloon you are making the molecules resist. Because the balloon and the molecules inside it are elastic, they will bounce back.

Now help your children fill a balloon with sand and another with water and see what happens. Does the balloon bounce now?

Explain that the special elastic properties of air makes it bounce, which is why tyres and sports balls are filled with air.

CASE MOTHS

We often find case moths in our garden and Andrew, our son, is fascinated by them. If your children find any in your garden, here is some interesting information about these fascinating creatures.

What You Need

- Case moths

What To Do

Case moths get their name from the protective case or bag in which the caterpillar lives. The case-moth caterpillar weaves the case with silk from its body and then covers the case with sticks, stems, and leaves to try to camouflage it.

The most common case moth in Australia is the Saunders case moth. Its case can grow up to 12 cm (5 in) long.

If the children hold the case moth carefully with the open end at the top, the insect may poke its head and legs out. They do this so they can move and feed. The caterpillar lives a year or more in the case before it changes into a moth. The female moth lays her eggs inside the case and, when they hatch, the young case-moth caterpillars leave the case via an opening in the lower end and immediately begin to make their own cases.

The case moth eats a variety of native plants, as well as roses and even pine tree needles.

COMMUNICATION LEGO

This activity tests your children's listening and communication skills.

What You Need

- Lego, Duplo or other construction toy pieces
- Two containers • Two children

What To Do

Sit the children back to back in the garden. Given them each a plastic container holding about fifteen Lego pieces. Each container needs to hold exactly the same Lego pieces—same shapes, colours, and so on.

One child is the 'communicator' and the other child is the 'listener'. The communicator begins to build something with the Lego and must tell the listener exactly what he is building. For example:

'I have taken a long green piece and I am putting a shorter red piece in the middle of it.'

The listener is allowed to ask questions to ensure she has really understood the communication. The game continues until all the pieces have been used.

Then the children compare what they have made to see how well they have communicated and listened.

COMMUNICATION PICTURES

Many thanks to my friend Lynne for this idea.
She uses it in her work as a School Guidance Officer.

What You Need

- Two children • Paper
- Coloured pencils, crayons or felt pens
- Clipboards

What To Do

The children balance their paper on a clipboard. They sit back to back with each other or in different parts of the garden, but close enough to communicate.

One child is chosen to be the 'communicator', the other is the 'listener'. The communicator begins to draw a picture, telling the other child exactly what she is doing. For example:

'I am drawing a sun with a yellow pen in the top left-hand corner of the page.'

The other child has to listen carefully and draw exactly the same thing on his paper.

The game continues until the pictures are complete and then the children compare pictures and see how well they have communicated.

COMPARING WEIGHTS

Young children often find it difficult to understand weight. This activity may help them realise weight and size do not always equate.

What You Need

- Two household bricks
- Short wide piece of wood
- Scales

What To Do

Walk around the garden with your children and find some things they would like to weigh and compare. You might find some wood, rocks, clumps of soil, feathers, different-sized leaves, flowers, and so on.

Balance the wood over the bricks like a see-saw and compare the weights. You can use your kitchen or bathroom scales to weigh the objects as well.

Compare some wet and dry objects too, such as wet and dry soil, or a wet and dry sponge.

COTTAGE GARDENS

If there's no room for a garden at your home, let the children make their own cottage gardens in besser bricks.

What You Need

- Besser bricks • Potting mix • Packets of seeds—petunias, marigolds, alyssium and other easy-to-grow flowering plants are ideal • Watering can

What To Do

Position the besser bricks in a sunny part of the garden because most annuals like full sun. Help the children fill the holes in the besser bricks with the potting mix. Water well. Sprinkle the seeds in the holes and cover lightly with more potting mix.

The children will enjoy watering their seeds daily and watching them grow. Some seedlings might have to be removed if they all grow—check the seed packet to see how closely they should be planted.

Extra seedlings can be planted in small pots. They make lovely gifts or are great to sell at school fetes or garage sales.

GARDEN RUBBINGS

4+

*This game will keep the children amused when you are working in the
garden—or when you want to sit down and have a few minutes to yourself!*

What You Need

- Paper • Crayons

What To Do

When the children aren't looking, go into the garden and do some rubbings—choose bricks,
pavers, tree trunks, leaves, grass, flowers or anything else that you can see.

Give the rubbings to your children and invite them to go on a rubbing hunt. Can they find the
original objects? When all the objects have been found, encourage the children to try their own
garden rubbings. Can they trick each other?

4+

GROWING STRAWBERRIES

Your children will love growing and eating their own strawberries.

What You Need

- Strawberry runners • Bale of hay

What To Do

In early autumn, enlist your children's help to dig a sunny garden bed for the strawberry plants. The soil should be loose and well drained. Add lots of animal manure and compost material.

Buy some strawberry runners. Help the children plant the runners in rows about 40 cm (15 in) apart.

Place straw around the plants so the berries will stay clean. The straw also helps keep the moisture in the ground.

Encourage the children to help look after their strawberry plants by watering and weeding, and they will be rewarded with delicious, juicy berries.

Hint!

If you live in a unit or space is restricted, buy a strawberry pot with holes in the side and plant your runners in this. You can still have a lovely crop of strawberries to enjoy with the kids.

GROWING SWEET PEAS

Sweet peas are lovely flowers, and they look and smell so beautiful when picked. Grow some with your children and they will love them, too.

What You Need

- Plastic pipes and connectors for a trellis
- Instant concrete • Chicken wire
- Sweet-pea seeds or seedlings • Compost

What To Do

Sweet peas are climbing plants and require a good-sized trellis. Make a simple trellis by joining lengths of PVC piping with corner curves to make a large U-shaped section. Concrete this into the ground with instant concrete. When the concrete's dry, attach the chicken wire. Another idea is to buy some plastic mesh and attach it to two strong garden stakes for the sweet peas to climb on.

Dig the garden bed well below the trellis and add lots of compost and organic fertiliser. Make sure it is in a sunny position as sweet peas need full sun and protection from wind. Leave for a few weeks.

If you are planting seeds rather than seedlings, soak the seeds in water for twenty-four hours before planting to hasten germination.

Have the children help you plant the seedlings or seeds. Water and feed them regularly, and in later winter and spring you will have beautiful climbing sweet peas with lots of pretty flowers.

GUINEA PIGS

Guinea pigs make terrific pets and can be great companions for young children.

What You Need

- Guinea pigs
- Hutch

What To Do

Guinea pigs are social creatures and it is always best to have at least two. (Choose two of the same sex unless you want lots of guinea pigs!)

Guinea pigs need a wire and wooden hutch to live in with a mesh floor to enable them to eat the grass. One part of the hutch needs to be enclosed so they can shelter and retreat for protection. They need to be kept warm and dry, and shredded newspaper or straw makes excellent bedding. This needs to be changed regularly (great for the compost bin!).

You can feed the guinea pigs special pellets, but they also need a wide variety of vegetables such as lettuce, carrots and pumpkin.

When the children handle them, make sure they support them with one hand under their body. If the guinea pigs are squeezed or held too tightly they may squeal or, occasionally, bite.

Warning!

Guinea pigs are fairly timid little animals and are often frightened by dogs, so if your family already has a dog, guinea pigs may not be for you.

Also, some children who suffer from asthma, skin allergies or hay fever may be allergic to guinea pigs.

HEATBEAT

Children are always fascinated by a doctor's stethoscope. Make a simple homemade version with your children and they can listen to each other's heartbeat and play 'doctors'.

What You Need

- 2 plastic funnels
- 1 m (3 ft) plastic tubing to fit the funnels

What To Do

The children can help you push a funnel into each end of the plastic tubing. Push as hard as possible so the funnels won't come out. Have one child place a funnel over her heart and the other funnel over her ear. Now she can listen to her heartbeat. (Jumping up and down a few times will increase her heartbeat and makes it easier to hear.) Let the children listen to each other's heartbeat.

Explain to your children that the heart is a large pump and the stethoscope is just a device to hear it better.

HERB GARDENS

Herb gardens are a wonderful addition to any home, and children will love helping to plant and care for a herb garden.

What You Need

- A sunny spot in the garden
- Punnets of herb seedlings, small plants or seeds

What To Do

Make sure the spot you choose for your herb garden has well-drained soil and receives lots of sunlight. If you have sandy soil, you will have to add lots of compost manure.

Decide with the children which herbs they would like to plant. I like to use fresh herbs in cooking and, therefore, try to make sure there are always herbs such as sage, parsley, rosemary and basil readily available. I also love the different mints.

Take the children to a nursery or botanical garden where they can look at and smell different herbs. The best way to smell a herb is to pick a leaf and squeeze it to release the aromatic oils.

When planting your seeds, remember that some herbs grow very large, so make sure there is enough room for the plant to grow.

The children will enjoy having their own scented herb garden and you will love having fresh herbs to use in your cooking!

HOUSEHOLD NOISES

An excellent listening activity that all the family will enjoy.

What You Need

- Tape recorder • Blank tape

What To Do

When you have some time on your own, go around the house taping different noises. You might include the bath emptying, the dog chewing a bone, the dishwasher or washing machine, the iron hissing, the door bell, the vacuum cleaner, the phone and the computer.

Play the tape back to your children and see how many sounds they can identify. Try out the rest of the family and see how well they listen. I bet that, unfortunately, they are not as familiar with the vacuum cleaner noise as Mum.

LETTERBOX SPOTTING

4+

My son and I like to look for different types of letterboxes as we walk. Try this with your children.

What You Need

- Time

What To Do

Go for a walk around your neighbourhood with your children. Try and spot different types of letterboxes. You'll be amazed how many varieties there are.

Talk to your children about the materials the letterboxes are made from, whether they think they would work well or not, and if they like them. See if they can recognise all the numbers they see on the letterboxes. Talk about odd and even numbers, and help them understand that the even numbers are on one side of the street and the odd numbers on the other.

Follow-up at home by asking your children to see if they can come up with a design for a different type of letterbox.

MAGNET FUN

Buy some magnets so your children can discover how they work.

What You Need

- Collection of small items made from different materials,
  such as buttons, coins, cutlery, hair clips, nails,
  pegs, safety pins, small toys, stones, sticks

What To Do

Explain to your children that magnets are made from a special sort of rock called magnetite and that they attract iron and steel. Give your children a pair of similar-strength magnets. Show them that magnets have two poles, a north and a south, and how magnets can repel and attract each other.

Now give your children a collection of small household items. Let your children try each item with the magnet to see which objects are attracted to the magnet and which are not.

Try to help your children understand that objects are pulled or attracted to the magnet, but they do not 'stick' like glue.

Have the children go around the house finding other items and appliances that are 'magnetic'.

Later they might enjoy a magnet 'treasure hunt'. Hide some small metal items in a dish of sand and they can each use a magnet to hunt for treasure in the sand.

NATIONAL PARKS

National Parks are natural treasures that we should value and utilise often.

What You Need

- Information about National Parks

What To Do

Find out more about the National Parks in your area. If you want to camp you will probably need permits, and some National Parks are so popular with campers that you may need to be placed on a list.

While families are encouraged to use and enjoy National Parks, we are also expected to be thoughtful and careful. The purpose of our National Parks is to protect the unique ecology of these areas. Visitors should avoid damaging vegetation, as well as any earth and rock formations. Try to keep to established roads and tracks and avoid cutting down trees or branches—even dead wood has a use in the bush.

Find out as much about the National Park and its special features and interests before you visit, to ensure your children will get as much out of the trip as possible.

Take plenty of photos. You must not take plants home with you, but the children can take paper and crayons for leaf, bark and rock rubbings. They can also draw some pictures of the wonderful things they see. These would be great with the photos for 'show and tell' or a special project at school.

NEIGHBOURHOOD PLAY MAT

*Make a play mat of your neighbourhood for your children
to use with their little cars and trucks. A great way to teach
simple mapping skills to young children.*

What You Need

- A sheet of heavy duty white vinyl
- Coloured permanent marking pens

What To Do

Discuss with your children the features of your neighbourhood—where the roads go, the houses, parks, local shops and any other familiar landmarks. Then carefully mark them on the vinyl (you might like to do it in pencil or coloured chalk first and then draw over it in permanent pen when you are happy with the result).

Mark your home, your neighbours' homes, the local streets and the landmarks on the map. Go for walks with your children and talk about other landmarks you could put on their map. When the map is made, let the children use it as a play mat.

OPPOSITES

*Go for a walk through the garden or a park with
your children and play the 'opposites' game.*

What You Need

- Time

What To Do

A child needs help to develop her language skills and to expand her vocabulary.

Go for a walk with your children and see if they can find something in the garden or park that feels bumpy. When they have found it, see if they can find another object that feels the opposite to bumpy.

Talk together about the words that would best describe the second object.

Next, ask them to find something that feels soft. Again, after feeling it, see if they can find something that feels the opposite to soft.

Try again with rough and spiky.

By the end of your walk, your children will have encountered several different textures and learnt some new words.

Keep the collected items. Your children may like to draw and label (with your help) some of the things they found.

OUTSIDE LISTENING GAME

Listening well is essential for good communication. We need to help build good listening skills in our young children before they begin school.

What You Need

- Tape recorder with batteries • Blank tape

What To Do

When your child is not around, tape some of the sounds you hear outside. You might tape:

Vehicles
The lawnmower or other garden tools
The dog barking, howling or scratching
Birds in the garden
Children playing next door
The sound of the sprinkler
Someone swimming in the pool
A wind chime

Play the tape to your child and see how many sounds he can identify. If he is having difficulty go outside with him and see if this helps.

4+

PATTERNING

Encourage your children to notice patterns in their environment.

What You Need

- Container or bucket • Cardboard • PVA glue
Materials such as: • Leaves
- Grasses • Flowers • Pebbles
- Small twigs • Bark

What To Do

Go for a walk through the garden or a local park with your children and collect some natural materials to use for making patterns.

Spread out the materials on an outdoor table and see if the children can use them to make patterns. If they are having difficulty with this concept, model some simple patterns for them such as:

Leaf-flower-leaf-flower-leaf—ask what comes next
Stone-bark-leaf-stone-bark—ask what comes next

See if the children can make some patterns of their own with the materials.

They may like to glue some of their patterns onto cardboard to keep and look at later.

SNAIL MYSTERIES

Do you have lots of snails in your garden? Children are fascinated by snails and they will love finding out how old the snails are.

What You Need

- Snails • A magnifying glass

What To Do

Carefully look at the snails under the magnifying glass. Can you see the rings on their shells? Count the rings on each snail's shell. The snail with the most rings is the oldest.

Explain to your children that as the snail grows inside its shell, the shell grows from the edge, and so more and more rings are added. Each ring means a growth spurt.

Trees have rings, too. Next time you see a log, see if you can count the growth rings and see how old the tree was.

SPRING-FLOWER PICTURES

A beautiful way to preserve spring flowers.

What You Need

- Small flowers and leaves • Iron
- Waxed or greaseproof paper
- Marking pen

What To Do

Go for a walk in your garden with your children and pick some flowers and leaves to make spring-flower pictures. Small flat flowers work best for this project.

Help your children arrange the flowers as artistically as they can on a piece of waxed paper. Then place another sheet of waxed paper on the top and iron carefully with a cool iron. The wax in the paper will bind together and seal the flowers inside.

Draw around the outside of the flowers with a thick marking pen—perhaps a heart or flower shape—and cut out.

The spring-flower pictures look great Blu-Tacked on windows or use them to decorate gift cards.

SPROUTING SEEDS

*Your children can help add variety to salads
and sandwiches by growing their own sprouts.*

What You Need

- Seeds such as alfalfa, lentils, mung beans, soy beans
  (best bought from a health food shop
  so you know they are free from chemicals)
- Cup • Strainer or colander • Large glass jar
- Piece of thin cloth such as muslin, cheese cloth, net
- Rubber band or elastic

What To Do

Help your children measure half a cup of seeds into a strainer. (For larger seeds use a colander.) Rinse well under running water. Pick out any damaged seeds and then place in the large jar. Pour in three cups of tepid water and leave to soak overnight.

Next morning rinse the seeds once more in the strainer, then return the seeds to the jar and cover with the fine cloth. Secure around the top with a strong rubber band or piece of elastic. At least three times a day rinse the seeds well by filling the jar with tap water and draining through the cloth. Keep the seeds in a cool dark place—the kitchen pantry is ideal.

In a few days the seeds will be ready to eat and you and your children can concoct some yummy salads for the family.

TEXTURE RUBBINGS

Develop your children's interest in their environment
by showing them how to do texture rubbings.

What You Need

- Paper • Crayons or pencils
- Textures around your house and garden

What To Do

Go on a 'texture hunt' with your children. Place the paper over car tyres, bark, leaves, carpet, coins, tiles, flowers, bricks and any other interesting textures you can think of. Your children then rub with their crayons or pencils. Label the textures rubbings for them so they can shown them to the rest of the family.

VISIT AN ART GALLERY

Most cities have numerous art galleries you can take your children to visit.

What You Need

- Time • Entry fee

What To Do

Take your children to visit art galleries in your local area.

Your children will enjoy seeing how other people portray the world. You may even notice that your children's drawings and paintings improve as a result of seeing this art. Follow up a visit by borrowing books about art and artists from your local library.

If any of your children show particular interest or talent in art find out about local art classes for them. We need to do all we can to foster our children's creativity and unique interests and talents.

WEATHER CHARTS

*Help your children build their knowledge of weather
and weather patterns by making a weather chart.*

What You Need

• Paper or cardboard • Calendar • Drawing tools

What To Do

Help your children draw up a large calendar for the month on a piece of paper or cardboard. Hang it in a place your children can easily access. At the end of each day, discuss with them what the weather was like, and they can take it in turns to draw the symbol or symbols for the weather in that day's square.

Use simple symbols for storms, rain, clouds, wind, sun and so on.

Look back at the end of the month and see what the weather pattern has been. The children will be enthralled by this activity. They will show much more interest in the weather report on the news and in unusual weather phenomena occurring in other parts of the world.

SPORTS
SKILLS

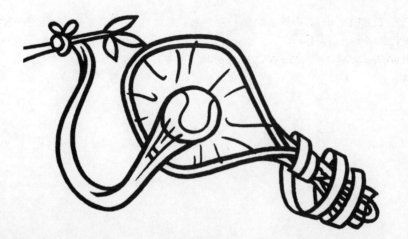

BALLOON FUN

Very young children love playing with helium-filled balloons.

What You Need

- A helium-filled balloon • A long string

What To Do

Tie a long string to a helium-filled balloon. Make sure the string is long enough so that your child can grab it when the balloon is resting against the ceiling. Your child will enjoy tugging on the string and making the balloon 'dance'. She'll also have fun pulling the balloon away from the ceiling, then letting go of the string and watching the balloon rise.

Dispose of any broken balloon parts promptly—always remember they are a choking hazard for young children.

BALLOON VOLLEYBALL

Blow up some balloons and let the children play this great game in the garden.

What You Need

- Balloons • Two or more players
- String or rope • Space to play

What To Do

Blow up several balloons (you'll only need one, but it may pop). String up a rope between two trees or posts and hit the balloon over the rope as in volleyball. Explain to the children that they must keep the balloon off the ground and hit it back over the rope. A player gets a point if his opponent doesn't stop the balloon from touching the ground.

Very young children will be happy to simply bat or push a balloon.

JUMP THE ROPE

A very young child cannot skip with a rope. However, fun rope activities like this will help develop your young child's coordination and balance.

What You Need

- A long rope

What To Do

It is fun for children to step or jump over a stationary rope. Tie one end to your clothes line and the other end to a tree or post. Have the children run up and step or jump over the rope. With young children make sure the rope is very low.

KICK THE BALLS

1+

*Encourage your child to push and kick different balls.
It's great for his coordination and muscle development.*

What You Need

- Balls of different sizes and shapes

What To Do

Set up a row of different balls in the backyard. Show your child how to go along the line and kick each one.

Line the balls up again and show your child how to push or throw each one.

Very young children love this game and will keep at it for a very long time. It will soon be obvious which of the balls is your child's favourite.

BOUNCING BALLS

Children love bouncing balls. Try this game with them and see if they can beat you.

What You Need

- Flat surface to bounce balls on
- Tennis balls or other soft, bouncy balls

What To Do

Count the number of times your children can bounce a ball in a row. Write down their scores so they can see if they can beat their PB (personal best).

When they can bounce really well, ask them to:

Bounce with their right hand only
Bounce with their left hand only
Alternate hands
Bounce twice with their right, then twice with their left, and so on
Bounce under their legs, right then left
Clap between bounces
Bounce high then low, and so on

CLOWN CAPERS

2+

Boxes make great toys—they are cheap, easy to obtain, and it doesn't matter if they are wrecked because you can always use another box.

What You Need

- A large cardboard carton • Masking tape
- Felt pens • Scissors or a craft knife
- A wooden box, stool or chair
- A brick or large book
- Soft balls or beanbags

What To Do

Use the masking tape to close all the sides of the box. Draw a funny clown's face with a very large mouth on a strong side of the box. Cut out the mouth with the scissors or craft knife and put the box on a chair outside. Put the brick or book inside the box to stop it falling over.

The children will love trying to 'feed' the clown with the balls or beanbags.

As their aim improves, make them stand a little further back. This will improve their throwing skills.

2

HOT DAY KNOCK 'EMS

When children's (and parents') tempers are frayed on a hot day, put the children in their swimming costumes and they will love a game of hot day knock 'ems.

What You Need

- Plastic bottles filled with water
- Large sponges • A table
- A bucket of water

What To Do

Line up the plastic bottles (without lids) on the table outside. Put the sponges in the bucket of water. Have the children take a sponge each and take it in turns to throw their wet sponges at the bottles. The aim is to knock down as many bottles as they can.

The children must drop their sponges in the bucket of water after their throw. That way the sponges will be really dripping when the children throw them. Soon, everybody will be dripping also, and much, much cooler and happier.

PING-PONG BALL ROLL

2+

Ping-pong balls are cheap and fun to use.
Make sure your children have a ready supply.

What You Need

- Ping-pong balls • Thick rope

What To Do

Have the children lie the rope along the ground and push it into interesting shapes, such as a circle, a squiggle, and so on. They now roll the ping-pong balls along the side of it. How quickly can they make the balls move without them shooting off?

This is a lot of fun. Have a go yourself!

SKITTLE KICK

We spend a lot of time teaching our children to catch and throw,
but it is also very important that they learn to kick balls.

What You Need
- Ten empty plastic two-litre milk bottles
- Water or sand • Medium-sized soft ball

What To Do

Half fill the plastic milk bottles with water or sand and screw the lids back on tight. These are the skittles.

Place the skittles on the ground in a V-shaped formation. Have four at the back, three, then two, and one at the front.

The children take it in turns to stand on a line that you've made and kick the ball at the skittles. The aim is to knock down as many skittles as possible with one kick.

Encourage the children to keep their scores on a blackboard or a large piece of paper. This way they'll be improving their counting as well as their kicking skills.

BIKES

Learning to ride a bike is an important part of childhood, and training wheels mean that even very young children can master two-wheeled bikes.

What You Need

- Bikes • Bike helmets • Food
- Water • Backpacks

What To Do

Take the family on a bike ride. It's safest to follow a bike track. Make sure all the bikes are in good condition and that everyone is wearing a bike helmet.

Your local council will be able to supply you with maps of the bike tracks in your area. Plan a family bicycle expedition—make sure you include the children in the planning.

Take some food and drink in backpacks for a picnic. Ensure everyone stops for rests and drinks. It's worth investing in water bottles that attach to the bikes so that everyone has their own.

Enjoy the scenery and the fresh air as you exercise together as a family!

Hint!

Even littlies can come along if you buy a baby seat for Mum or Dad's bike. Make sure baby has a helmet, too!

3

BUCKET TARGETS

Develop your children's throwing skills with a simple game of bucket targets.

What You Need

- A plastic bucket
- Tennis or other soft balls, or beanbags
- A brick

What To Do

Place the bucket on the ground at an angle, propped up by the house brick, so the bucket is tipped towards the throwers. Mark a spot where the children must stand, and let them take it in turns throwing the balls into the bucket. Handicap older children by making them stand further away from the bucket than the littlies.

Ask the children to record their scores on some paper or a blackboard.

If the bucket is too small a target for younger children, a plastic garbage bin makes an excellent target, or perhaps a plastic laundry basket.

HOT POTATO

A simple throwing game to play with a group of children.

What You Need

- Children • A medium-sized soft ball

What To Do

The children join hands to form a circle and then drop their hands.

Give one child a ball to start the game. Ask the children to pretend that the ball is a sizzling hot potato, so when they get the ball, they have to pass it to the next player in the circle as quickly as they can. This game is fast and furious and great fun!

OUTDOOR PLAY EQUIPMENT

Outdoor play develops muscles, strength and coordination.

What You Need

• Plastic rubbish bins • Outdoor equipment

What To Do

Provide your children with an assortment of outdoor play equipment. This will help develop the muscles and strength they will need for school.

Suggestions include:

A variety of balls, plus a bike pump and needle to keep them inflated

A variety of bats

A trampoline or a rebounding mat

A totem tennis set

A net to kick balls into

A basketball hoop set at the appropriate level

Skipping ropes—a long one and individual ones

A quoit set

A plastic golf set

I have found a couple of plastic rubbish bins to be ideal for storing all this equipment; one for bats, one for balls etc. Check the bins regularly to make sure there are no 'nasties', such as spiders, lurking in there.

THE PEG GAME

*Children need many opportunities to develop fine motor skills
and the muscles needed for holding pencils and writing at school.
This game helps develop those skills in a fun way.*

What You Need

- Clothes pegs that open and close
- Clothes airer or thin cord or rope
- Two containers

What To Do

Organise a peg game with the children. Put ten clothes pegs into each container and set up a clothes airer. Alternatively, tie a length of thin cord or rope between two trees at the children's waist level.

The children stand on either side of the airer or at either end of the rope. When you say 'go' they put their pegs onto the line as fast as they can using only one hand. (Ask them to hold the other hand behind their back so they are not tempted to use it!)

The first child to secure all their pegs on the line is the winner. If you have lots of children organise them into two teams for a relay. The first child in each team puts the pegs on the line, then runs back and taps the next child's hand. That child then takes the pegs off. He then runs back and taps the next player and she puts them back on, and so on.

Challenge the best 'pegger' to a game against Mum or Dad.

PING-PONG BALL BLOW

If you have some space at home, a ping-pong table is a great investment. Children can also get hours of fun just out of ping-pong balls.

What You Need

- Ping-pong balls
- Two or more players
- Large table

What To Do

Have two children, one at each end or side of a large table or flat surface, take it in turns to try and blow a ping-pong ball past each other. They have to be goalkeepers and try to defend their end by blowing the ball back to the other end or side.

This is hilarious to watch and much harder to do than it sounds!

PING-PONG BALL HOCKEY

This is another fun ping-pong ball game.

What You Need

- Ping-pong ball
- Rolled-up newspapers or cardboard cylinders
- Two cardboard boxes • Two or more players

What To Do

The children make 'hockey sticks' out of the rolled-up newspapers or two long cardboard cylinders. They place two cardboard boxes on their sides at both ends of the garden—these are the goals.

If there are two players, then each child tries to use her 'hockey stick' to tap the ping-pong ball along the ground, past their opponent and into her goal. If there are more than two players, make teams.

TRAMPOLINING

Children love bouncing on trampolines, but make sure your children are properly supervised because many accidents occur on trampolines each year.

What You Need

One of the following:
- A trampoline • A rebounder
- An inner tube from a tractor tyre covered with canvas and laced together underneath
- An old foam mat or mattress

What To Do

The trampolining area should be clear from obstructions, such as tree branches, clothes line, or anything lying underneath or near the trampoline. The springs should be covered with purpose-made padded mats. Check the springs are all connected and working and that the trampoline is on a level surface. Trampolines are only safe for one person at a time. Children should wear suitable clothing with no buttons, zips, buckles, shoes or jewellery. Long hair should be tied back.

Unfortunately, many spinal injuries occur each year on trampolines, so make sure your children warm-up first by stretching and bending to loosen their back muscles. Show the children how to sit down and safely slide off the trampoline.

When children begin bouncing it should always be in a still and stable position, and sessions of about three to five minutes are best. Discourage knee drops as they are dangerous and can easily cause spinal injuries and whiplash. If your children are keen to do more on the trampoline, let them join a gym or trampoline association.

WISHING-WELL TARGET

3+

Make a wishing-well target in the garden. Your children will love throwing 'coins' into it and making a wish. This is also a great idea for a party, special event or fundraiser.

What You Need

- Two large cardboard boxes • Scissors • Strong tape
- A large plastic dish or tub • House paint
- Stones • A tin of gold spray paint • Aluminium foil

What To Do

Cut a circle out of the bottom of a large cardboard box. Fit the dish in the circle. Make the top of the wishing well out of another box with strong cardboard supports to hold it up. Paint the wishing well and decorate it with glitter, flower cut-outs, fairies or anything else that takes your fancy.

Spray some pebbles or small stones with gold paint or cover them with aluminium foil. The children will love throwing their 'coins' into the wishing well and making a wish.

This idea is great for the fairy birthday parties that are so popular with little girls.

BOX TARGET

4+

*Visit your local electrical store and ask them for a large computer,
stove or television box to make into a throwing target.*

What You Need

• A large box • A craft knife • Insulating tape
• Beanbags or old socks filled with rice, dried beans or sand • Balls

What To Do

Carefully cut shapes from different sides of the box. Use a variety of shapes, such as squares, triangles, diamonds and rectangles. Cut some shapes large and others small. Cut some shapes at ground level and some higher in the box.

Edge the shapes with different-coloured insulating tape for strength and to make them stand out.

Cut a trapdoor in one side of the box, so the children can retrieve the thrown items easily.

Give the children a variety of different balls and beanbags to throw. They will enjoy throwing the objects through the holes. This will develop their aiming skills.

Older children can enhance their numeracy skills by writing down everyone's scores and keeping a running total.

CHALK TARGETS

This simple game will provide hours of fun and lots of practice at throwing. Children need good throwing skills for games at school and organised sport.

What You Need

- Coloured chalk
- A wall that is suitable for throwing against
- Saucer • Balls or beanbags

What To Do

Use chalk to mark a large circle on a wall of the house. In the middle of the circle mark a red target—trace around a saucer to make a perfectly round circle.

The children stand a few paces away. A hoop makes a good circle to stand in or else mark it with some of the chalk.

They score ten or twenty points when they hit the red target (the bull's-eye) and five or ten when they hit within the bigger circle.

As they become more proficient at hitting the target, make them stand further away. Handicap older children by making them stand further away than the littlies!

Give the children some paper and pencils to keep score, or let them score on the concrete or pavers with the chalk—it will just hose off when they have finished!

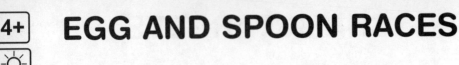

EGG AND SPOON RACES

Great fun for birthday parties or whenever you have a few children together.

What You Need

- Teaspoons (plastic ones work well)
- Golf balls • Starting and finishing lines

What To Do

Each child has a teaspoon and an old golf ball to balance on it. They line up at the starting line. When you say 'go', they start racing.

The children must keep one hand behind their back at all times to resist the temptation to hold the ball on the spoon. The aim of the game is to walk or run as quickly as possible to the finishing line while still keeping the golf ball on the spoon.

If a child drops the ball he must go back to the starting line and begin again.

This game is a little like the old story of the hare and the tortoise—slow and steady usually wins this race!

HURDLING

*Children love running and jumping and you can set up
a simple hurdling track easily in your own backyard.*

What You Need

- Empty three-litre juice tins • Can opener
- Broom handles • A bag of instant concrete
- House paint • Ropes

What To Do

Ask your friends to collect three-litre juice tins. Take the lids off using a can opener that leaves a smooth top. Buy some broom handles from a hardware store or supermarket and a bag of instant concrete. Fill each tin with the concrete and push a broom handle into the middle of each one and hold it straight until the concrete begins to set. Leave them for a few days to harden and then the children will enjoy helping you paint them.

Set up the hurdle course by tying ropes between the juice-tin broom handles for the children to hurdle over.

SCOOP BALL

Playing this cheap and simple game will help your children develop the visual tracking skills they need to play many types of sport.

What You Need

- Two-litre plastic milk or juice bottles with handles
- Craft knife or scissors • Masking or insulation tape
- Tennis or other small soft balls

What To Do

With a craft knife or sharp scissors cut the bottoms off the plastic milk or juice bottles. Tape over the sharp edges with some masking or insulating tape.

Hold the scoops by the handles and use them to catch and throw balls to your children. This game is not only lots of fun but also develops your children's hand-eye coordination as they move their scoops to catch the ball. Also, it develops their skills at visually tracking a moving object. Children need these skills later to play sports such as tennis, hockey, cricket and baseball.

SKIPPING RHYMES

*As children gain mastery over skipping with a rope they love
to learn skipping rhymes to skip to. You may know some
from your own childhood that you can pass on to your own kids.
If not, here are some that I have used with young children.*

What You Need

- A long rope of medium thickness

What To Do

Turn the rope and chant the rhymes as your children skip. A great winter's day activity to warm everyone up.

Mrs Pink fell down the sink.
How many litres did she drink?
1, 2, 3, 4, 5, 6, 7 (and so on).

This one is excellent for teaching the letters of the alphabet.

Apple pie, cherry tart, tell me the name of your sweetheart.
A, B, C, D, E, F (and so on).

The children stop skipping on any letter they wish. If it is D, they think of a name of a child of the opposite sex whose name starts with D. Perhaps:

Donna, Donna, come to tea. Donna, Donna, marry me?
Yes, No, Yes, No, Yes, No (and so on, until they are out).

If they are proficient skippers swing the rope faster and faster until it is pepper!

SKIPPING WITH ROPES

Skipping is a great skill for children to master.

What You Need

- A long rope of medium thickness

What To Do

If you don't have another adult or an older child around to hold the other end of the rope, tie one end securely to the clothes line or a tree. Show your child how to stand on one side of the stationary rope and ask him to jump up and down and land with both feet together. (This will be difficult for many four-year-olds.) As he jumps, turn the rope to fit in with his jumping rhythm.

If he is still having problems, stand with him, hold both his hands and jump together saying 'jump, jump, jump', until he has grasped the idea. Sometimes letting a child see another child skipping helps, too.

As your child gains confidence his skipping rhythm will become more even. He may find it difficult at first to fit in the extra little jump as the rope turns above his head, but this comes with time. When your child has learnt to skip with a long rope, he will enjoy skipping on his own with an individual skipping rope, but make sure it is not too long for him or it will trip him up.

I have often found that boys are reluctant to learn to skip as they perceive it as a girls' game. You can overcome this by pointing out that most footballers and many other male athletes skip regularly to stay fit. In fact, most boys really benefit from learning to skip, so do persist with your sons!

TIN-CAN CLIP CLOPS

*Help your children make some simple stilts from tins
and watch them walk tall around the yard.*

What You Need

- Two large empty soup tins of the same size
- Clothes line or other thin rope • Acrylic paint
- Hammer • Nails

What To Do

The children can help scrub the tins to remove the labels. Use the hammer and nail to punch two holes in the side of each tin very close to the filled-in end.

Now the children can paint the tins in bright colours with some acrylic paints. (Some paint manufacturers now sell small sample tins of paint that are ideal for projects like this.)

When the paint is dry, measure and cut the rope to fit the children. String a piece through each tin and tie a good-sized knot in both ends so it can't come out.

The children stand on the tins and hold onto the ropes tightly as they walk on their tin stilts. This is very hard for some children and they will need to practise.

SPECIAL
OCCASIONS

BIRTHDAY THANK-YOU CARDS

Make some gorgeous thank-you cards using a cute photo of your child.

What You Need

- Coloured cardboard • Coloured pens
- Reprints or photocopies of a photo of your child
- Scissors • Glue

What To Do

Here's a great way of saying thank you to all those people who have given your child birthday presents.

Fold sheets of coloured cardboard in half. Let your child decorate them, even if it's only a few wild squiggles. Glue a photo of your child on the right-hand side of the cardboard. Cut a shape out of the cardboard on the left-hand side, make sure it's over the photo when the cardboard is folded, so the photo can now be seen.

Write a few words of thanks inside the card and pop it in an envelope.

EASTER-EGG HUNTS

Make it a little harder for the children to find what the Easter bunny has left with an egg hunt on Easter morning.

What You Need

- Small Easter eggs
- A basket, bag or dish for each child

What To Do

Rise early before the children and lock up your dog (so he can't eat the eggs before the children find them).

Hide the eggs in the garden, but in fairly obvious places so the children can find them. Make sure you know how many you have hidden.

Gather the children. Give each one a basket or bag to put their eggs in, then let the egg hunt begin!

Make it a rule that the children can only eat a couple of Easter eggs in the morning, and must save the rest for later. That way you'll avoid upset tummies!

HUNT THE EASTER BUNNY

Childhood is so short and so very precious. Your littlies will love hunting the Easter bunny on Easter morning, and you'll enjoy watching them do it!

What You Need

- A small basket of Easter eggs • Flour

What To Do

Get up before the children and dip the knuckles of your index and middle fingers in some flour. Now make 'bunny footprints' through the house and out into the garden. Give the children quite a trail to follow and at the end—wow!—a basket of eggs.

The amazing part about this activity is that someone always spots the Easter bunny while you are following his trail!

LIVING CHRISTMAS TREES

Instead of having an artificial Christmas tree, plant a living Christmas tree that you can bring indoors every year at Christmas time.

What You Need

- A small Norfolk pine or other conifer
- Large pot • Potting mix

What To Do

Visit your local nursery or a nursery specialising in conifers. Do this some months before Christmas as there will be a much better selection, and they are usually cheaper then, too.

Buy some fresh potting mix and a large pot in which to plant your Christmas tree. Don't forget to ask where's the best place to put the pot in your garden, and if your tree has any special requirements.

Look after your tree all year and the children will enjoy having a live tree to decorate at Christmas time.

BIRTHDAY TABLECLOTH

Have your child make a special tablecloth for her next birthday party.

What You Need

- Large sheets of paper
- Paints and coloured pencils
- Sticky tape • Clear plastic tablecloth

What To Do

Let your child decorate the large sheets of paper any way she likes. She may like to include lots of birthday images, such as a birthday cake, candles, gifts and party food. She should decorate as many sheets as you need to cover the table.

Tape the sheets of paper together and place over the table. Cover the paper with a clear plastic tablecloth.

CHRISTMAS CARDS

Encourage your children's creativity and give them a holiday activity by making wonderful Christmas cards for friends, family and neighbours.

What You Need

- White cardboard • Red and green acrylic or poster paint
- Small brushes or potatoes for printing • Ice-cube tray
- Takeaway plastic containers • Kitchen sponges
- Glitter • Hole punch

What To Do

Begin by cutting the cardboard. If the cards are to be posted, make sure they will fit comfortably into white envelopes. If they are to go with gifts, cut small rectangles or squares to attach as gift tags. The children will enjoy helping you cut the cards and punching a hole in the corner of the gift tags.

If the children want to print, help them cut Christmas shapes from potatoes—stars, trees, bells etc. Put some red and green paint in plastic takeaway containers and they can carefully push the shape into the paint and then print with it. They'll love sprinkling on some glitter while the paint is still wet.

If they want to paint their own Christmas pictures, put some paint into ice-cube trays. After they've painted the cards, they can add some glitter as a festive touch.

CHRISTMAS CROWNS

*Let your children make their own Christmas party crowns this year.
They will prefer to wear them at the dinner table, rather than
the ones in Christmas crackers (which are usually far too big for
young children's heads).*

What You Need

- Measuring tape • Pencil • Scissors
- Art smock or old shirt • Newspaper
- Powder paints • Brushes • Stapler

What To Do

First, measure around your children's heads to work out the size of the crowns. Allow an extra 5 cm (2 in) for joining. Cut strips of cardboard 15 cm (6 in) wide and the appropriate length after measuring. Now carefully cut a zigzag along the top of each cardboard strip, to make the points of each crown.

Now your children can have some fun! Cover a table with newspaper and give the children an art smock or old shirt to wear. Then let them paint the crowns in their favourite colours. Encourage them to do some Christmassy designs on their crowns. Put the crowns aside for several hours until they are completely dry.

When the crowns are dry, wrap them around your children's head, and make a small mark with a pencil at the point where they need to be stapled. Then staple the crowns together. Your children will be very proud to wear their own Christmas crowns at the dinner table on Christmas day!

3+ CHRISTMAS PAPER CHAINS

Decorate the house for Christmas or a special occasion with old-fashioned paper chains. They not only look festive, but they are a fun way for your children to improve their cutting skills and learn how to use a stapler.

What You Need

- Scrap paper (old wrapping paper looks bright)
- Ruler • Scissors • Stapler

What To Do

Lay the sheets of scrap paper on a table. Help your children use a ruler to draw a mark every 5 cm (2 in) along the base of each sheet. Cut up along the marks. It's best if the paper strips are no longer than 20 cm (8 in).

Take a paper strip and fold it over to form a loop and then staple. Remind your children to always place the stapler flat on a table and to press it down hard with both hands until they hear two clicks. Stapling needs quite a lot of hand strength, so help your children and be patient!

Put another paper strip through the loop and staple, and so on, until the paper chain is as long as you need.

Hang the chain up together and admire the results of their hard work.

CHRISTMAS TWIG TREE

*Go for a bush walk with your children and collect lots
of twigs to make a different sort of Christmas tree.*

What You Need

- Milk carton (cut in half—use the bottom section)
- Quick-set plaster (available from hardware stores)
- Christmas fabric or hessian • Ribbon • Twigs

What To Do

Place the twigs in the milk-carton bottom. Arrange them so they form a balanced shape. Carefully pour in the plaster and allow it to set. Wrap the Christmas fabric or hessian around the milk carton and tie with a contrasting bow.

Your children will have lots of fun helping you decorate your Christmas twig tree. It looks great 'au naturel', but it can also be sprayed with gold or silver paint for a very pretty effect.

COLOURED EASTER EGGS

*Make some brightly coloured Easter eggs with the
children to use as Easter decorations around the house.*

What You Need

- Art smocks • Plastic containers
- Food colouring or powder paints
- Water • Spoons • Hard-boiled or blown white eggs
- Birthday candles • Masking tape • Paper towels

What To Do

Put the children in their art smocks, then make up some strong solutions of water and food colouring in the containers. Have a spoon for each container.

The children carefully draw interesting patterns in wax (with the birthday candles) on their eggs. If you are using blown eggs remind them to be gentle as the eggshells are fairly delicate. Now dip an egg into a colour and then take it out carefully and wipe dry.

If the children want to have multi-coloured eggs, wrap some masking tape around sections of each egg before dipping it. Then, remove some of the masking tape and dip into a second colour. Repeat the procedure until the egg is multi-coloured with interesting designs.

The eggs will look beautiful on the table for Easter lunch. (Remember not to eat these hard-boiled eggs!)

LETTERS TO SANTA

Help your children write and post letters to Santa Claus. Secretly write and send replies, so your children have the excitement of receiving a letter each.

What You Need

- Paper • Pencils and drawing pens
- Envelope • Stamp • Scissors (optional)
- Toy catalogues (optional)

What To Do

Talk about Santa with your children. Tell them that Santa would love to get letters from them. You'll need to do the writing, but your children can tell you what to write. Then, they can draw pictures of themselves, the family and your home to include with the letters.

Next, they might like to draw or cut out from toy catalogues the things they would like from Santa. I always stress to my son that Santa can only bring one large present and fill his stocking, as Santa has lots of children to deliver to and we must share.

Finally, address the letters and your children can stick on the stamps. Walk to the mailbox together to post them.

Make sure the replies come in a few days as young children find it very difficult to wait for special things!

MAKE A FLAG

Make your country's flag.

What You Need

- Paper • Paints and coloured pencils
- Strips of coloured paper • Glue
- Dowel • Sticky tape

What To Do

On your country's national day, make your country's flag with your children.

Show your children an illustration of your country's flag. Explain the significance of the parts of the flag and suggest that you make one together.

Help them decorate their cardboard flag with paints or coloured pencils, or they may like to tear up and glue on strips of coloured paper.

When it's finished, tape the flag to a short piece of dowel and display it proudly.

ST VALENTINE'S DAY CARD

3+

Valentine's Day is 14 February and it is traditionally the day for lovers.
Make some Valentine cards with your children for them to give to special people.

What You Need

- Red or pink cardboard • Pencil • Scissors • Strong glue
- Decorations such as ribbon, lace, pretty stickers • Flowers

What To Do

Draw some large hearts on the pieces of cardboard and your children can cut them out. The hearts are the cards. Let your children decorate them any way they like.

Help younger children write on the back of their hearts, older children can write their own messages.

Your children may like to sign their cards, but traditionally Valentine cards are anonymous! Deliver the Valentines together!

AUSTRALIA DAY

Help your children learn more about Australian customs and traditions.

What You Need

- Green and yellow crepe paper
- Gum branches • Australia Day food

What To Do

Australia Day on 26 January commemorates the day in 1788 when the First Fleet landed in Sydney Cove. It is an Australian holiday and most towns and cities have Australia Day picnics or celebrations. Why not go to one with the family or have an Australia Day barbecue at home?

Your children can help you make green and yellow streamers from crepe paper and they can gather gum branches to decorate the barbecue area.

Serve traditional bush fare, such as barbecued chops, sausages and damper, followed by pavlova and a good strong cup of billy tea. If you want to be more adventurous, many Aussie bush foods are now available in specialty shops.

Have some competitions after lunch, such as horseshoe throwing or a tug of war. Maybe you could sing songs like 'Waltzing Matilda' or the 'Wild Colonial Boy', or have a poetry reading with some of Banjo Patterson's poems—great Aussie entertainment!

CHRISTMAS CLAY CENTREPIECES

These simple, cheap clay ornaments make great Christmas presents.

What You Need

- Clay • Candles • Leaves, seedpods, wheat, grasses
- Gold or silver spray paint (optional)
- Christmas tartan ribbon (optional)
- Florist wire (optional)

What To Do

Help the children manipulate the clay into a large, flattish round base. The base needs to be high enough to hold the stems of the leaves and other decorations. Smooth the base, then add the decorations, making sure they are pushed in firmly. If you are going to keep the centrepiece 'au naturel', simply add the candles and place the base in a safe place in the sun to dry for a day or so.

If the children want to spray their centrepiece gold or silver, the candles will have to be taken out. Because the clay shrinks a little when dried, make sure the holes for the candles are a little bigger than the actual candles. Do this by helping the children place the candles in the clay in the required positions and then wiggling them around a little before removing them.

When the clay is dry, you can spray the centrepiece. Make sure you put lots of paper underneath it and only spray on a still day. When the paint is dry, replace the candles and help the children make some tartan bows and secure them in place with florist wire.

FATHER'S DAY BOTTLES

Teach your children the pleasure of giving by making a special gift for Dad on Father's Day.

What You Need

- An attractive glass jar
- Glass paints (available at craft shops)
- Fine brushes or cotton buds
- Goodies to go in the jar

What To Do

If you have an interesting glass jar, use that, or else visit your local 'junk' shop—they often sell nice chunky glass jars with cork lids.

Buy some bright pots of glass paint from your local craft shop. This special paint won't wash off when you wash the jar.

Your children paint on the design, then you fire the painted bottle in the oven (follow the directions on your paint pot).

When the bottle is cool, fill it with Dad's (or Grandpa's!) favourite sweets.

HOLIDAY SCRAPBOOK

A great way to keep family holiday memories alive.

What You Need

- Scrapbook • Glue
- Photos and holiday mementos
- Drawing and writing materials

What To Do

While you are on holidays, save all the memorabilia, such as train tickets, fun park entries, postcards and photos. (When you have your holiday snaps developed, have doubles made—one set for your children's holiday scrapbook and the other set for the family photo album.)

Assemble all the mementos and photos (pick a rainy day to do this) and glue them in the scrapbook in chronological order—a good memory activity. Encourage your children to draw some pictures about the holiday in the scrapbook. You or your older children can write the captions.

Older children can write a story about the best thing they did on their holiday, while younger children can dictate their story for you to write. You may be surprised—our child spent a night in a small country hospital after a fall on our last holiday and that was the highlight for him!

MOTHER'S DAY SURPRISE

Your children will love creating this simple
jewellery box to give to Mum on Mother's Day.

What You Need

- Newspaper • Art smocks • Shoebox with lid
- Acrylic paints • Brushes • Felt • Glue

What To Do

Cover an outside table with newspaper, then put the shoebox and paints on it. While you're doing this, your children can be putting on their art smocks.

Let the children paint the shoebox and lid in a light colour—pale yellow looks nice. Allow the box to dry.

Now, let the children decorate the box any way they like. They may like to pick a theme, such as the beach or wild animals.

Once the paint has dried, line the inside of the box with felt—glue it in place.

Wrap the jewellery box in colourful wrapping paper and give it to Mum.

SANTA FACES

*This easy-to-make Santa is a great decoration for your
child to hang in his room at Christmas time.*

What You Need

- Round paper plate • Marker pens
- Red cellophane or crepe paper
- Scissors • Glue • Cotton wool

What To Do

First, have your child draw a smiling Santa face, right in the middle of a paper plate. Make sure he leaves room on the plate for Santa's hat and his cotton-wool beard.

Now cut triangles of cellophane or crepe paper out for Santa's hat. Help your child to stick the hat on to the paper plate. Next, he spreads glue along the bottom of the plate and around Santa's mouth. Then he sticks cotton wool on to the glue—this is Santa's beard. If your child likes, he can also put a dab of glue on the tip of Santa's hat, and put a blob of cotton wool on that too!

Put Santa aside for a few hours, while the glue dries. Your child will proudly hang his artwork up, for a very festive look.

ST VALENTINE'S DAY POSIES

Help the children make some flower posies to give to their
teachers or special friends on St Valentine's Day (14 February).

What You Need

- Small flowers • Ferns • Cardboard
- Coloured pencils, crayons or felt pens
- Hole punch • Aluminium foil • Ribbon

What To Do

On the day before St Valentine's Day walk around the garden together and pick some small dainty
flowers and ferns or other greenery. Leave the plants to soak in water overnight.

Cut some card into small heart shapes and the children will enjoy decorating them. Let them write
their own messages if possible or, if they are still too small to write, you could do this for them.

The next morning, before kindergarten, pre-school or school, help your children assemble their
posies. Wrap the base of each posy in aluminium foil. Punch a hole in each heart card and thread
some pretty ribbon through the holes. Tie a card to each posy.

Help your children deliver their special floral Valentines.

ZANY BIRTHDAY POSTERS

4+

These zany and colourful posters look fabulous and are so much fun to make.

What You Need

• White cardboard or thick paper • Coloured paint
• Paintbrushes • Black crayons • Hairpin

What To Do

Have each child entirely cover a piece of cardboard or paper in squares of painted colour. The squares of colour must be applied thickly. Allow to dry.

When this is done, each child must entirely cover the piece of cardboard or paper with black crayon. The black crayon covers the squares of colour.

Now each child uses a pointy implement (e.g. hairpin, end of a paintbrush) to scrap a large birthday message in the black crayon. As the child scraps away the paint, the coloured crayon will appear from underneath.

You'll be surprised how terrific the poster looks. Display the poster above the party table.

ACTIVITY INDEX

383